GROWTH

An Inmate's Guide to Inner Corrections

by

Craig A. Byrnes

GROWTH
An Inmate's Guide to Inner Corrections

You may access other books by Craig A. Byrnes at Amazon.com

Or contact Craig at:

Craig@inmatesguidetocorrections.com

ISBN: 978-1-98-600804-4

This book is dedicated to George.

If not for you, this experiential writing project would not exist.

I celebrate the awakening of your soul and send

compassion, kindness, joy and balance

out to you on the breath!

In the west,

people will respect the name of the Lord;

in the east, they will glorify him.

For he will come like a raging flood tide

driven by the breath of the Lord.

Isaiah 59:19 (NLT)

A NOTE TO READERS…

Incarceration can be a spiritual experiment laboratory where we can test our ability to create new ways of acting, while watching our thinking process with new eyes. If you're not currently in a correctional facility, my suggestion is that you work the books anyway to see where it takes you. If your thinking mind is truly the problem, it makes no difference where you are for awakening to happen.

RECOMMENDATIONS FOR THE MEDITATIVE JOURNEY

- Work on balance, not right or wrong.
- Be honest with yourself.
- It's okay not to know.
- Be gentle with yourself.
- Live in the present moment.
- Set small goals for yourself along the way.

GOAL EXAMPLES

- Physical exercises.
- Simple eating habits.
- Mental exercises.
- Emotional development exercises.
- Spiritual exercises.

HELPFUL DEFINITIONS

- Prayer – talking to God
- Meditation – listening to God
- Ego – that which looks out for self only.
- AM – higher self.

The time to change is now! The past is over and the future cannot be controlled. The key to action is to change our mind's awareness of the possibilities.

A VERY IMPORTANT FINAL NOTE!

This book will have repetitive concepts ON PURPOSE. I'm asking that you join me in practicing both the readings and the principles each day with the intent of applying them to your life. This book provides a vehicle to an expansive consciousness that goes beyond that of the ego-driven mind. I'm blessed that you even took the time to pick the book up and read this far. May you find serenity in your own journey.

January 1st

Whether we've been down a few days, or a few years, New Year's Day is a holistic day to start fresh with resolutions to change our lives. This is a day to say "YES" and discover who we are underneath all we do. Rather than concentrating on changing all of our bad habits (by making a list of New Year's Resolutions), why not come to know who we are by making a decision to turn toward the direction of the process. We can begin by observing the pieces of ourselves. Finding out who we are is a continuous process, not a destination. The commitment to this process takes courage. The focus changes from an exterior solution to an internal one. We will start by meditating for five minutes and add one minute each day until we reach a minimum of forty minutes. Now is the moment to start practicing the benefits of meditation as a means to illuminate a larger perspective other than "me, me, and me."

I make a decision to start with five minutes a day and to increase my practice one minute each day, until the 35th day, for a total of forty minutes of meditation. In order to make a permanent change in life, we must practice a new behavior for more than thirty days to increase the chance that any transformation will last long term.

The only place I can depend on to actually do my meditation is my bed. I start my practice by experimenting with observing my body and senses. I begin by sitting on the outside edge of my bed, with legs relaxed, back straight, and hands resting comfortably (on the top of my legs) upon my knees. My eyes are open, gazing outward and my mouth is slightly open. I start engaging with my meditation seat by taking a look at my five senses, beginning with my sense of feeling the physical. I think in order, from my head to my shoulders, and downward to my chest (feeling my heartbeat). I sense my stomach and then focus on where my seat meets the bed. I concentrate on my legs - my thighs, knees, calves, and extending down to my ankles. Finally, I come to discover how my feet feel on the floor.

Once I observe the sense of touch throughout my body, making sure my posture is erect, yet relaxed and open, I start to discover only the sense of sight. Lowering my head, just slightly, so that my gaze is aimed at the floor, I try not to focus on any specific point. I notice the linoleum is tan with spots.

Next, I change my focal point to the sense of hearing. I choose the morning to experiment because the noises are minimal. There are sounds of a toilet flushing, someone snoring down the hall and a single set of footsteps.

I explore the sense of taste. It isn't so much about what I can taste. It is about focusing on how my tongue savors whatever is in my mouth at the time.

Finally, I move on and embrace the sense of smell. The mustiness of the unit is evident, along with the smells coming from the bathroom across the hall.

I expand to change my focus to my breath. I breathe in and out and beyond, celebrating the movement of air in my lungs.

At this point, it isn't long before the first thoughts start to invade my solitude. I have read plenty of material on meditation. I found a precise, yet gentle, way of dealing with my mind's activity from a suggestion by Pema Chodron. Looking at the thoughts precisely, yet also very gently, I just say the word "thinking" aloud and go back to my breath.

Now it's your turn. These are my meditative notes. I encourage you to keep a journal and do the same, writing your own notes about your experiences through meditation.

January 2nd

Let's go back to the days of school. You're sitting at a desk and staring out the window, either daydreaming or being carried away by something we view outside. Without warning, you hear your name being called, along with the stern words: "PAY ATTENTION!" Remember those days?

Now that we're on the second day of our commitment to sit and get to know who we are, we can ask the question, "Just exactly what does "paying attention" look like?"

We have all learned, at some point, how to tie our shoes. Later on, we can chew gum, have a conversation, or listen to music while we do this task. The act of tying our shoes is no longer a conscious action. To tie our shoes consciously (in the present moment) is a very different type of activity. Normal shoe tying relies on a memory of the past. When we memorize something, we move it to our subconscious.

Let's try tying our shoes with the idea of thoughtfulness. More precisely, putting our shoes on, taking both shoe laces in each forefinger and thumb (left and right), crossing the laces over and under and pulling the laces to tighten them. It makes no difference whether the left lace goes over the right or vice versa. Once the laces are crossed and pulled tight, make a bunny ear with one lace. Again, it makes no difference if it's the left or the right lace. Then, make a bunny ear with the other, and hold them in each hand touching side to side. Making another choice, cross one bunny ear over the other, and then under, pushing the bunny ear into the hole and then pull. The lace is now tied. It takes total concentration to tie shoes this way - unless this is the way you have already learned.

What we're experiencing is the idea of precision. It's right there in the present moment - stark and harsh. Now, we have the opportunity to do something totally different. Meditation allows us the leeway to add the soft and slow action

of compassion and kindness to ourselves. These concepts may not stick right away, so we will have to continue practicing being compassionate and kind to ourselves without any expectations. This is the third element of meditation - the action of being open. We will come back to these three ideas (precision, compassion, and openness) over and over again.

Today is the day to add one more minute to meditation, moving to six minutes. I take my seat on the bed to explore my body and my posture. I move through to sight, hearing, taste, and smell. What I really work consciously on, today, is how to be gentle and compassionate about the thoughts that keep carrying me away. Speaking the word, "thinking," about a thought seems to be the best way to be kind to myself. I am recognizing the thought is there, yet softly bringing myself back to the present moment of my breath. To be thoughtless is not the goal. This is going to be a process, not an end product. I successfully meditate for six minutes, with thoughts rising and falling, and go on with my day.

January 3rd

Wisdom comes out of each moment. Whether we call it the Holy Spirit, the wisdom mind, the space, the nature of the Buddha, or the quantum physics arena, this place is still the same. It is accessed by allowing the acceptance of thoughts and knowledge of the mind, while turning our egos over to this power that is greater than ourselves. We are dropping away our thinking.

We don't control this force. It flows through us like the wind through the trees. We can't see it, but we come to know it is where we consciously practice letting go.

This wisdom is not positive or negative; for that is a description used in this world - the universal duality. Truth is often a paradox. The first are last and the last are first. Underneath all the sorrow that exists, inside a living human body, is the light of unconditional love and being. Jesus said it plainly, "The Father and I are one." Perhaps he was simply saying, "I AM."

Without all the materialism of religiosity, we can sit fresh in the present moment and experience "I AM," even if we are not to do it perfectly every moment of our lives. We can keep coming back to the present. It is where we are conscious of our breath.

In sitting quietly and listening to this wisdom of power, there lies the energy of compassion waiting for discovery. All we have to do is be willing to ask and sit for the consciousness of wisdom to enter us in its own time. This is the process of accepting now, while being courageous.

Sitting for seven minutes is the task I commit myself to today. I take my seat. I check my posture and explore my body from head to toe. I observe my gaze. I change my focus to my hearing, then move to the taste of peanut butter and honey in my mouth. I go right from being curious over my sense of smell to just my breath. The thoughts that arise during my meditation consist of where I would live and what I would do to support myself when I get out of prison. Gently, I just say, "thinking," and go back to my breath.

Once I finish my seven minutes, I realize the wisdom of where I will live and what I will do to support myself (when I get out) are thoughts for the future. Coming back to my breath is a compassionate gesture bestowed upon me from my wisdom mind. I can do nothing about those questions now. What I can do is stick to my commitment to meditate - to place myself in the position to move closer to my acceptance of wisdom.

January 4th

In our commitment to sit and look at who we are, and what is in front of us, we are combining the physical world with the spiritual energy that gives us life. We become an experiment in quieting what we do, so we can experience the wisdom of intuition. This process forces us to become more intimate with who we are.

We are not human doings; we are human beings. Meditation is a practice that allows us the chance to see what "not doing" can accomplish in the balanced relationship between our actions and our sense of consciousness. To begin, we don't open to the vastness of the Universe. The focus is too broad.

In sitting meditation, we find that focusing inward and quieting the mind allows us to examine life from the inside out. This is something our thoughts may keep us from doing. Our goal is not to collect wisdom as some prize, but instead, to allow it to flow through us as we are.

Another spiritual principle comes to fruition as we sit. We are in this world, but we are not of this world. We cannot experience the spiritual realm without the ability to be physical. We are allowed to choose the option to seek the spiritual, while being physical. It is not mandated.

Our physical properties need the spiritual energy that gives us life, and our spirituality needs our physical mass to make this choice. In the midst of this relationship is the balance of intuition and wisdom. We come to know God is because we are.

Again, the goal in meditation is not to define God. That is impossible! This spiritual power defines us over and over and over again as we come to understand, in each breath, a present moment experience.

Today is the day for eight minutes of meditation. It's time to take my seat, become conscious of my willingness to examine my body's uprightness, be aware of the senses of sight, hearing, taste and smell, all bringing me to my breath. I have to repeatedly evaluate my posture and return to my breath.

To sit and become aware of my mind and body, and then the value of my consciousness is the initiation to cultivating a new way of living. I have to develop the patience to sit and just be, while continuing to come back to the breath, by saying the word, "thinking."

I also have to come to grips with how distracted I am by various voices within the unit that draw me away from my practice. Through meditation, I have become acutely aware of how distracted I can become when I hear someone else's voice.

If I am going to continue to be open to this process, I have to let go of the voice on the outside, the same way as I do on the inside. What comes to me, after my session, is the word "repent."

Casting aside the traditional Christian understanding of this word, I consciously look at the roots of what the word means: think again. Instead of physical thinking (what I naturally would do with my ego), I am attempting to listen to the higher voice inside me. This is higher thinking. I have to turn inward for this solution. This is the voice of intuition that acts through me, expanding outward. Today is a practice of letting go and letting God. It is also a day of recognizing progress, not perfection. Perfection is a spiritual disease; one where the goal is to control an outcome. I have become acutely aware that outcomes are in the future. Coming back to my breath is indicative of leaving the past and the future behind to deal with feelings head on - while continually letting go of the voices inside and out.

January 5th

In our search inward, we can come to see that what we do, how old we are, and what we feel changes from moment to moment. What doesn't change is who we are. The force that gives us life is constant and the ultimate in consciousness.

By starting with who we are, we become grounded and connected to that which gives everything life. Let's not get all bogged down in the religiosity of trying to pigeonhole this force. Instead, let us start by making a decision to give more space to our narrowed experience of tender-loving kindness. Moving away from the idea of receiving some sort of rewarding for what we do, let's turn towards honing in and sitting with the sensation of tender-loving-kindness from the space of who we are.

As we breathe in, we can take in all of the stressful sensations that we encounter within each moment of meditation through all of our senses (sight, sound, smell, taste and physical sensations). We can combine them with whatever emotion arises and breathe out tender-loving-kindness.

The more space we give to each moment as we sit, the greater our experience to sense tender-loving-kindness. If we don't know what this sensation feels like, we just focus on giving more space to our practice. We don't force tender-loving-kindness; it comes to us by offering our vulnerability. The experience comes to flow naturally, from who we are, in its own time.

Today is the day for nine minutes of meditation. Bringing my physical self to my seat on the bed, exploring my posture clearly, while gently moving through my other senses (sight, sound, taste and smell), brings me to a whirlwind of thoughts.

Seeing them clearly, and then letting them go, by saying, "thinking," urges me to be open to the idea of tender-loving-kindness.

The thoughts I have to let go:

- I really wanted chocolate cake yesterday for lunch. I have made a decision to give up sugar while being incarcerated. A Monster drink is one of the pieces of the puzzle that brought me to this present moment, so stimulants are now off the menu.
- One of my roommates is selling soft porn. I am not happy about this. Enough said.
- The general noise of the unit is a challenge for my meditation practice and I am distracted over and over again.

I have let go of these thoughts gently. I find this challenging. What wisdom I walk away with today is: I am not very kind to myself. Yet, just practicing letting go of the thoughts, while sitting with the emotions of fear, anger and shame, has to be enough for today. Even the thought, "I am not kind to myself," I treat like a meditation thought – and say "thinking." I let it go.

Letting go is tender-loving-kindness to me. This new behavior is not smooth and it doesn't have to be. I have to remind myself this is a process, not a destination.

Wanting chocolate cake, disliking being exposed to seeing my roommate sell soft porn to others and the daily noise that occurs during my meditation are not permanent predicaments. Later in the day these thoughts and my feelings about them dissolve. What I think about never stays the same. Only who I am remains constant. This is a new idea to embrace. I have to practice hope that this process will stick and then let go.

January 6th

The world needs more compassion. It starts within. It is nurtured in an environment where we are all connected. The common definition of compassion is not the goal. The goal is to see what is.

In order to heal our lives, this focus inward brings us to a great place of sadness. Having compassion for ourselves begins with going to the space created by meditation; this act starts the healing in our lives. We go to take our seat and we find ourselves between the two audiences of incarceration - the inmates and the correctional staff. We must let go of the idea of blame.

We can begin the grieving process suggested to us by Elizabeth Kubler Ross. She shows us how to explore the five stages of grief:

- **Denial that we have a problem.**
- **Anger that comes from facing the truth of what is.**
- **Bargaining and procrastination that steers our focus away from taking personal responsibility for our feelings.**
- **Sadness.**
- **Acceptance that allows us to practice compassion. Being empathetic with ourselves helps us to open to our hearts in three distinctive ways. First, we become the individuals who are in the process of awakening in the midst of those feelings, letting go of those thoughts. We expand our consciousness, which brings us to compassion. Second, we start to expose ourselves to the spiritual teachings of cosmic law - limitless principles of pure truth and wisdom. And third, we seek out connection to the others on the path of spiritual growth.**

Here we begin to become curious about being conscious of the present moment and how this consciousness allows us to let go of blame and sit with emotions that freely arise. We are committed to the path of educating ourselves to open our

hearts to the creation of compassion. We introduce our commitment to the path of service - commencing with ourselves.

Today is the day of ten minutes of meditation. By taking my seat, I start my pledge towards starting each new day fresh. Without judgment, just saying "thinking" and letting go of each thought, I begin to see how most of my thoughts are about either reliving the past or trying to figure out what is going to happen in the future. By gently stopping those thoughts and returning to my breath, I can once again experience what is happening now.

In the moment, I can see the root of my urge to fix the past or control the future is meant to take me away from the process of the grief I feel about being incarcerated. Staying in the now of my breath is proceeding away from denial, and allowing me to feel the sensations of anger and fear rising inside me. Even though I continue to drift away in my thoughts of the past and future, bargaining my way out of dealing with this experience, I have begun to sow the seeds of compassion in the garden of my soul.

Meditation is the fertilizer needed to create compassion for myself - to heal my broken heart. Feeling the sadness, that comes with being locked up, opens my heart to acceptance through compassion. What a huge project! Staying in the moment, I remind myself that it is done one day at a time; sometimes one moment at a time.

January 7th

Bringing natural peace and joy into our lives takes willingness. Creating a space for that peace is a decision based on choice. If we let go of trying to control the Universe (with what we believe is right), we can experience the path to familiarity with this undefined source of power that comes from life itself.

Whatever we're feeling or thinking, we just recognize what is there, without the need to change a thing. Going inside and focusing on the breath, taking in all that is, we come to the present moment where all peace and joy flow. Relying on compassion and kindness, we can open ourselves to the process that has no beginning or end.

My commitment to meditate eleven minutes today is strong. Once I've finished, I go to work. Because of my sincere work ethic, I've always done my best to prepare for tasks in advance. If I can get something started early, I can take the time to see all that has to be done. I can strategize a plan, and then, it's full steam ahead to achieve the goals I have set.

Fortunately, I have found, through meditation, that if my ego is in control of the undertaking, I become aware of my need to grasp and command the consequences of my efforts.

Today happens to be a day I work alone at my job station. I prepared the day's schedule yesterday. All I need to do is go through the motions of follow-up to make sure there are no errors.

Upon posting the roster for the evening and the following day's shift, I plunge into the next self-appointed chore. There are various employee charts that need to be updated. Finding the appropriate people and getting the necessary signatures is a challenge. Over 265 people work in food service.

While getting initials and signatures, I discover there are pay sheets that have not been signed from the month before. I start to push myself to get both tasks done at the same time. Separating those pay sheets that have already been signed takes a while. Meanwhile, the lunch meal has started. I forego standing in line to save time.

I ask one of the cooks for a sandwich, eating it hurriedly, while sorting the pay sheets. I am mid-stream in my toil, when suddenly I am gripped with the consciousness that I am not peaceful. In fact, I am aggravated that time has crept up so quickly, making completion of employee charts and payroll sheets impossible. Plus, I am stuffing my food, as an act of self-hatred.

Suddenly I pause and breathe, trying to allow space for the wisdom of joy and peace to fill me. This is not an easy task; however, over and over, I keep reestablishing the moment with a restful pause. I see this gap, accepting that my ego is fighting to take over the outcome of self-assigned responsibility.

When I over perform, I don't create peace and joy. I create more fear, and consequently, I speed up to control and avoid pain. But, in placing my sights on the completion of tasks as a goal, I destroy the center of serenity from which I should operate.

Finally, I let go of the idea that all the day shift payroll sheets are going to get signed today. Instead, I allow the target of sorting all the sheets, prepared and ready for easy signing, to be enough. I continue to stop and start my day with the breath of peace and joy, allowing it to flow from the expanse of the slow breaths I take from time to time.

After lunch, I locate an officer to remind him that he agreed to help me with the venture of making over 850 copies of various forms for new inmate orientations. I receive this granted gift of grace. In the library, the ambience for peace brings me to continue my afternoon meditation, while standing and collecting all the duplicates at the copier. Reacting overly responsible (or irresponsibly) sows the seeds of chaos, not peace. Performing the rite of peace and joy takes courageous determination that starts with my conscious breath.

January 8th

We are born to our first breath. There will never be an inhaled breath without an exhalation. In meditation, we become aware of this balance of opposites. We always return from whence we came. The spiritual term for balance is equanimity.

As we practice today, let's feel the cycle of breathing akin to the movement of the tides ebb and flow. Then, if we start thinking, wandering away from our awareness of the breath, we can accept the contemplation and come back to the center of balance. We focus our awareness again on the breath.

Prison is judgment. Someone does the judging and our sentence is imposed. There is black and white, up and down, in and out. Everything in the physical world has an opposite, just as the breath of meditation. When we turn to meditation we're turning away from our thoughts. Perhaps the lion's share of our thoughts center on who is to blame for our every moment of incarceration.

Meditation takes us out of our heads and into our hearts - the core, the center of our being. Here there is no blame, only the flowing of emotions and the sensations they create on our visceral journey inward.

There is a learned man among us. He knows who is right and who is wrong. He judges the man who has only completed a 3rd grade education, his inability to do a hard day's work and the criticism he utters towards everyone and everything which speaks of his superiority.

I'm reminded, by his commentaries, to keep myself centered where the breath is. I can remember my days of self-righteous pride, when whatever I spoke was the truth. What a folly that was and still is. I'm sure my days of sitting in the judgment seat are not over. Judging is as out of balance on the coin-of-missing-the-mark as any other thing that causes transgression.

The focus of balance means watching my thoughts and giving them the space that my breath provides, so that balance can be stored naturally. Today, when this intellectual man judges me, when I don't reach his standard of perfection, I have the opportunity to pause and forgive him for his fastidiousness. If I have spoken a foul word, I can apologize, place guilt on the altar of absolution, and turn to the breath of equanimity.

January 9th

Only we know where our mind is today. We can either be in full drive with our obsessive thoughts, aggressive urges, yearning for something or someone, totally nonchalant, or simply remain dull inside our thought processes.

Wherever we are, we have the opportunity, on the cushion, to *know* where we are. We are the only ones who can recognize how our mind is doing today. No one can do that for us.

Once we have identified where we are, we can use that point to move toward the center of our being. This is working with the process of steadying the mind. We begin to work with our compulsive thoughts, not what is happening outside of our control. We identify what dissatisfies us and gently become present to identify what inside us is out of balance.

Being present allows us to become empowered. This is not achieved through allowing our ego to be in control of the present moment. We can begin to learn how to see, hear, smell, taste, sense, or think without being carried away by discursive thoughts driven by the past or the future.

I can identify the feeling of hopelessness today. It covers my entire body. It makes my heart beat harder at times. I am carried away by the thoughts of the past and the future. I work on being present, coming back to my breath. I do my best to feel hopelessness, without carrying on a conversation within to solve my unease.

I find it very difficult to sit with hopelessness, being distracted over and over. My mind is wild. I must keep coming back to my breath. My skin itches. I find myself scratching. The annoying sensation moves all over my body. I do my best to at least wait a few seconds, being present for the itch, before physically scratching any particular area of my body.

After meditation, my first thought is a comparison. I am training my mind to weight lift, just as I would my muscles. I begin to understand the idea of composing myself, no matter how my meditation starts. It doesn't matter how I am. There need be no critique. All I need to do is practice being more gradually conscious than I have been before I began my session. I recognize where I am, allowing the Universe to do the rest. My breath is the safeguard that allows me to rest in my soul, my inner being.

January 10th

In being with the breath, the object of our abiding is sensing the air flowing inward and outward. Pondering or scrutinizing the breath is not the goal. To do so moves us toward the idea of "thinking" about the breath. The idea is just to be with the breath, not to identify with it.

We meditate with our eyes open. The idea is to integrate our meditative practice with what is actually going on in the world around us. To shut our eyes is to compartmentalize our meditation into some sort of ideal. This separates us from being able to be in the world, while we practice being in the present moment.

Perhaps we can begin to discover some small "aha" moments, either in our practice or once we leave. Every single session is impermanent. They are all different. It's not whether our meditation practice is good or bad, fluid or stuck, but whether we are observing our thoughts, feelings and sensations, along with sights, sounds and smells all around us.

I become acutely aware of two levels of consciousness after my meditation practice:

- I do too much work for others.
- I confuse the criticism of what I do with who I am.

Fear drives my need to take on too much responsibility. In the present moment, I can just become aware of my fear. Shame is what I feel when someone criticizes what I do, instead of the feeling of guilt. "What I do is wrong," gets translated, by me, as "Who I am is wrong!" That idea fuels my need to do more to make up for the deficiency. My meditation practice allows me to let go of the scrutiny of these two issues, allowing me to start with where I am in the present moment. Whatever I have done in the past, I don't need to catastrophize. Coming back to the breath, being in the now, means being gentle with myself without blaming inward or outward.

January 11th

While journeying on our practice of meditation, we can add (to the clear-seeing aspect we've been working on so far), the characteristic of gentleness and relaxation. Too much tightness in our concentration can actually increase our discursive thoughts. Too loose a concentration and our practice becomes dull. We may never experience the true transformative power that comes with balance between these two states.

Concentrating on the basics of attentive clear-seeing, we can add simple tender relaxation to balance our routine.

1. **Gently experience the inward breath.**
2. **Gently explore the body and feeling states.**
3. **Gently become aware of discursive thought, labeling it "thinking."**
4. **Gently exhale, letting go and letting God.**

This is another genre of meditation. It is not the ultimate, correct way to practice. Right and wrong is not the goal here. Adding friendliness to whatever format we're using allows us to act in a way that connects us to who we are. The path is the goal, not the destination, of peaceful existence. Perfection is never achieved, yet our balance between clear-seeing and gentleness may bring us to less suffering than an ego driven life. The powerful force that changes our lives only exists "NOW!" The present moment brings us to the possibility of wisdom. We let go of the idea of what's in it for our ego.

By exploring inwardly, we are performing an act that is called: cleaning *only* our side of the street! Through this practice (we have now reached fifteen minutes of meditation), we are inventorying ourselves. Through gently discovering our

good and bad points, we find a middle path that rises above the understanding of the physical realm.

Adding gentleness to my daily life, I make a decision to clearly see one of my strongest character defects: not asking for help. Concentrating on my breath, I put all of my handwritten book entries into a large envelope and mail them to Rod. I feel fear in asking him to make a copy of every page, then sending back the copies, while keeping the originals. My thoughts concerning the future are about his reaction to my asking him to help me with this project. Coming gently back to the present moment, I come to believe in the courageousness of my actions. The outcome is not in the present moment. Gently coming back to my breath, I exhale and place enough stamps on the package to carry it to its destination. Thinking about how to finish the book is also not "NOW!" Focusing on my inward and outward breaths, I place the envelope on the outgoing mail desk in the correctional staff office. Then, I warmly let go, staying with the process, staying in the spaciousness of being.

January 12th

Whether we're inside a correctional facility, or wandering around in a fog of rumination on the street, we can all treat our meditation practice like "freshly baked bread!" There's a spaciousness to experiencing the smell of bread right out of the oven. The opposite would be treating our practice like a stale product. Knowledge is not the focus, as that's not fresh. "Thinking" is about the past or the future. The present moment is the bread of our practice, coming right out of the oven, all fresh and demanding the kind of attention that brings us peaceful joy. This is the path to wisdom, which does not need thought.

A fresh curious approach, neither judgmental, craving, nor unconscious, allows us to be open to the central place within that brings us insight. We don't make it a goal to throw out our bodies, trying to reach some sort of nirvana. Instead, we bring our internal selves, while being a "watcher" who connects us to what we do. We research what moves us from the center of serenity, not striving toward goodness or away from bad.

Letting go and letting God is about leaving a roominess for the Universe to speak to us about its wisdom. We do this by continuing to return to the breath, over and over. In little bits and pieces, we gain the understanding of how letting go of our ego's desire to control outcomes allows our Higher Inner Self to bring us to the sanity of serenity.

I have two choices while living in a correctional facility. I can spend my sentence totally unconscious, full of resentment, doing my best to get even with the system that put me here, or I can surrender to the process and be curious about what it could offer me. I choose the latter. The wisdom in that choice comes in experimenting with the entire meditational path. Letting go of what I want, allowing the space of silence to appear in the midst of all my "thinking," allows me to become more comfortable with the uncertainty of day-to-day life here. I make a conscious choice not to play the victim role, but to reserve time every single day to rise above my ego's perceived adversaries and practice empowerment through meditation. Do I still "think" my way into dissatisfaction most days? Sure I do! Am I making progress at creating a new path? Absolutely! I just have to stop and smell the bread coming out of the oven.

January 13th

Pain is a part of our physical existence. Most of us, through compulsive thought, focus on the negative aspects of life, not the positive. There lies the problem. We don't have a larger understanding of pain. We have to surrender to a larger perspective. We evolve through pain when we become conscious of its greater purpose.

Insanity is doing the same thing, over and over, expecting a different result. The question I can ask myself is: "Why am I dissatisfied?" Then, I bring that question into my practice. With patience (and a dash of whimsy), the answer comes to me. My ego's view is limited. Everyone feels pain! It's not just me. We all share this in common. Pain connects all of us!

The solution, in our meditative practice, is to invite the pain in without fueling it with our ruminations. We make it our practice, by saying "thinking," to focus instead on the rawness of what we perceive as negative emotion. Once we truly own the energy of emotion, our inner awareness can shower us with compassion and tender-loving-kindness. Once we experience the healing, we can extend that to others who are in the same boat.

I examine suffering from a spiritual point of view, using my physical ability to act, to move me to a higher level of understanding.

My inner self alone can't act. It needs the physical me. Yet, I'm imperfect. I need to accept that too. I need my internal spiritual-self to achieve progressive wisdom.

I'm dissatisfied when my focus is on the physical alone because I spend the majority of my day in discursive thought. Is this inherently sinful? I go back to the spiritual root of this word, which translates as missing the mark. The physical me experiences duality, both positive and negative. Both of these aspects pull me in either direction, causing an imbalance. Therefore, I miss the mark.

With a spiritual outlook, I can live in the physical world, while holding my balance with the wisdom that all humanity suffers. I'm not alone. Through my acting meditative practice, I can focus on the spiritual center of just "being". Through love I am able to go back to the garden of eternal life.

I only need my imperfect physical self to act in the present moment, gently turning away from "thinking". The Christian Bible calls this "the bread of life." Transformation becomes possible through this path. I come to hit the mark above the realm of time and space. This takes courage and faith.

January 14th

Anchoring our consciousness in the present moment can be advanced by continuing to add all the senses of our human existence. Exploring sight, sound, smell, taste, and the sense of physical feeling further enhances our rooting in the "NOW". Once we add a particular sense to our practice, we may later alternate and combine these perceptions with the breath.

Let us begin with the sense of sight. When we have started our session, checking our posture and being with our breath, we launch our opportunity to be with color, texture, and brightness. There is no evaluation, only the realization of what we see. Our gaze may be short or long, high or low. If we start to contemplate what we are viewing, we can gently stop by saying the word, "thinking", and secure ourselves again.

The recreation yard is quiet in the middle of winter (and that is a thought, so I go back to seeing). I see my breath, as steam, close up. The vapor dissipates quickly, until the next exhalation. I am one with the moisture as it leads my gaze further out. I come to see the mountains, along with a patchwork of gray tree sticks and the mosaic of evergreens that extend for miles. The only movement is the clouds as they dance over the highlands, casting their shadows over the grayness. The blue sky is one with the clouds. The sun appears in and out of the clouds, moving forward and back to embrace the mountains as it continues to set. My first sight of it is yellow, then orange, and finally the sun turns to red as it slides behind the ridge.

The blue sky becomes yellow at sunset above the skyline. The clouds take on a pink and gray hue. I make the decision to continue my practice, to be with the process. The atmosphere expresses its twilight. The clouds become a muddy patchwork over the stubble of trees on the mountains. Darker and darker the colors become; the dimming summit swallows the trees until there is no detail. I go back to my breath. On the move, I walk back to my unit in silence.

January 15th

Nature abhors a vacuum. The idea of adding the consciousness of our senses to the practice is not to eliminate thought altogether. That's impossible. Including the senses purely moves us to the path of stabilizing our minds.

Sound is abundant in a correctional facility, or in a busy daily life on the outside. Funny, it's as prevalent as discursive thought is in our heads. In our practice, we season our consciousness with the friendly acquisition of the noises around us, moving away from evaluating what we hear. We focus on another part of our inner selves.

This is the process of coming to know a life above thoughts, giving up control, developing willingness as a life skill. Just as we come to discover thought (by labeling it "thinking"), we approach what we hear by being present for it. Being with the sound of silence connects us with the space of being.

I choose the library to work with sound. This is not a silent place; however, it has less volume than most places within my life on the compound.

Of course, my attention to the breath becomes distracted, not only by my thinking, but also by other low rumbling conversations at the many tables. It isn't long before I become attentive to the thought, "*I am easily drawn away by voices, my own or others. I am aware of how I put excessive value on what other people say!*" These are thoughts, so I say "thinking." I continue to train in listening to the voices without being lured away by my judgment.

Underneath the conversations are a host of other sounds to behold:

- The turning of pages.
- The squeaking or movement of chairs and tables.
- The clicks and hums of the copy machine.
- A singular cough.
- The sound of footsteps in all directions.
- Doors opening and closing.
- The sound of the mechanics of a stapler.
- The sliding of a book from and back to its shelf.
- The dropping of various objects on tables.

I become aware of the wisdom that it's not the sounds that are the issue. It is what my mind does, once it starts creating a story about the noises I hear. Just coming back to listening, closer and further away, strengthens my sense of being. It is another way of experiencing a connection to the present moment.

I move to a vacant classroom to continue my practice for a few more minutes and to hear what I can perceive. With the sound of the closing door, I can hear my heart beat. This brings me right to my breath. My heartbeat and my breath are always there. I'm here to listen to both and settle in. I realize I am distracted by all the other noises, leaving no room for me to be aware of either. Again, that's a thought, so I just go back and try again.

January 16th

Today, our meditation time expands to twenty minutes. Let's explore expanding our meditative practice by adding the sense of smell. We're not attempting to give any value to particular odors or scents. These types of words or notions won't help us to experience a present smell. We simply invite whatever smell meets us into the present moment. If our bodies react, we notice that, as well, and continue to go back to the act of smelling. If we get carried away, "thinking" about any particular item we've smelled, we can recognize that and come back gently to the act of smelling in general.

Different places have either an abundance of, or a limited set of offerings. We certainly have plenty of time, if incarcerated, to investigate many different environments. We can smell the dining hall, the microwave room in the unit, the church sanctuary, the library, the rec yard or inside the gym. Our own living spaces contain a plethora of smells. It's not about where we choose to go; it's about preparing an open mind in the midst of our choices, wherever we happen to be.

Since I work in the dining hall, I can take the time to meditate between meals. Without the room being full of humans, there is a greater sense of quiet in which to experience smells. I make the choice to do walking meditation, instead of sitting on my bed or in a chair. Being with my breath, while walking slowly, I replace focusing on my footsteps with whatever enters my sense of smell.

The office where I work has a mixture of lingering food smells that enter the office through the door. The vegetable steamer is right outside. The smell of paper and the mustiness of the enclosed office mingle with the scent of canned green beans.

As I walk out of the office and to the left, I eventually come to the locked doors of the bakery. I stop and place my nose near the space between the doors. The odor of paint is there and an even stronger presence of the scent of rising dough. The bread for the evening is not yet in the oven, so a strong scent of the yeast is breathing out as I'm breathing in. Both the dough and I are in meditation together. I am aware of the connection. We are both with the breath of respiration.

Leaving the bakery, I walk toward the compartment sink where the dishwashers are still finishing up pans from the previous meal. Inside the trash cans, near the sink, I have the opportunity to savor what has been scraped off of the pans before washing. Chicken grease, mixed with the smell of canned corn is inside. Moving toward the sink, I experience the food-scented steam mixing with the detergent in the first compartment of the sink.

Again, the smell of baked chicken grease rises from the foam of the soap. I become distracted when a comical inmate scoops up a handful of bubbles and blows them in my face as he laughs. As I come back to only smells, I am aware of the scent of his body, as he extends his arms toward me to blow the foam. "*Inmate so and so needs a bath*," is a thought, but I choose to go back to the smells for a moment longer. Then, I move on.

The dishwashing machine room is through the doorway. Another inmate is sanitizing the washed pans and metal trays by loading them into the dishwasher. These are the same dishes that were cleaned in the compartment sink. I notice a difference in the scent of the detergent used in the automatic dishwashing machine. The sound of the machine is like discursive thought, pulling me away from my focus. I come back to the sense of smell, noticing the scent of hot rubber. It is coming from the latex gloves the inmate is using to stack the pans exiting the machine.

Leaving the dish room, I receive a sniff of wax being buffed into a section of the floor in the dining hall. I take a seat close by to finish my session. I practice coming back to the smell of the wax, away from the discursive chatter of the sound of the buffing machine.

I’m very sensitive to any type of smell. But, that’s a thought. I keep going back to what passes through my nasal sensors.

January 17th

By bringing the sense of taste into our practice of consciousness, we can become aware that when we eat, our mind is usually racing. We're also not at the point of nirvana where we can be one with every single moment of taste. With that in mind, we'll have to take the middle road and practice by repetitively returning to the sense of taste.

Without having to go to the library to study the tongue, we can simply experiment with what we put in our mouths. The tongue has places where we are conscious of sweetness. Sour, bitter, and salty have places to be discovered on the tongue as well. The key is to be curious and explore each experience.

If we get distracted by any value given to a specific object, we must return to the act of taste, itself, and gently let go of the thought by labeling it thinking.

The dining hall is a great place to discover the sense of taste; however, it is also a place of powerful distractions. Since I'm just starting my practice of being in the present moment with taste, I choose my bed and three simple items to savor: peanut butter, peppermint tea and honey. These are things I buy at the commissary, as a way of being compassionate to myself.

I make a cup of tea in my plastic mug (there is a hot water dispenser in the unit), then I add honey from the little bear-shaped squeeze bottle and I open the jar of peanut butter. I take my seat on the bed, set my posture, turn inside to my breath, and slowly add sips and spoonfuls of my chosen foods of compassion.

A sip of peppermint tea and honey helps me to explore where I taste sweetness and spice. My sense of smell really adds to the experience, so I find it difficult to separate the two senses while tasting the peppermint on my tongue. The vapor fills my nose. I take my time getting into my practice, which causes the temperature of my tea to register as not too hot or too cold, but just right! If I concentrate on my breath and the taste of peppermint, the smell anchors me into the present moment. Practicing three levels of consciousness at once makes it difficult to have a thought.

The sweetness of the honey makes the peppermint smoother. Again, another thought. I'm just here to be with the honey and the tea. The two places on my tongue where I'm conscious of sweet and spice just are.

I put the spoon in the peanut butter and slide it into my mouth. My tongue spreads it out and the taste of peppermint and honey are muted by its thickness and earthiness. The peanut butter is colder on my tongue. That's a feeling sensation. Wow, a fourth dimension of consciousness to behold at once! Peanut butter is sweet and nutty. It's smooth.

I take a sip of tea and the heat of the liquid strips my tongue, allowing me to cleanse my palette and swallow. I take another sip to savor the sting of the spice with the nectar of the honey syrup. The closer I get to the bottom of the mug, the sweeter the mixture becomes. Honey is slow to dissolve, even in hot tea. That's a thought, so I go back to savoring the experience by tasting another spoonful of peanut butter.

January 18th

Our next level of consciousness is the state of physical sensation. We are continuing to strengthen our practice further. First, go back to January 1st and review the six points of reference to our bodies. Then, begin by taking a seat, legs relaxed, adjusting your posture, placing your hands on your knees, bringing your gaze to the front with eyes open, while allowing your mouth to let the air flow.

There is so much you can do by being with your body. Keep it straight forward as you begin. Start at the top of your head and go down, or bring your awareness to your feet and toes and go up. The focus is *not* where you start. It is just becoming aware of the different parts of your body. You're not judging how your body feels. Just be conscious of each body part, as you move up and down your inner self.

I observe the six points when taking my seat. I am in touch with my breath. Once I am at a point where I say "thinking" to any mind chatter, and my mind becomes stable, I start at the top of my head. The point is to range over my body, sensing the energy of what it feels like in that area:

- top of my head
- my ears
- my eyes
- my nose

- my mouth and tongue
- my throat (swallow)
- my chest (rises and falls with each breath)
- my shoulders
- down my arms to each hand and each finger (the sensation of my hands on my knees)
- back up my arms and down to my gut
- where my gut meets my seat
- my seat upon the bed
- my thighs against the frame of the bed
- my knees (the sensation of my knees supporting my hands)
- down each leg to my feet
- the feeling of my feet on the floor, then my toes individually

Now, back up.

I let go of any conversation I may desire to have, as to what I am sensing in my body. The process isn't simple or difficult. It just is.

January 19th

Meditation allows us to observe and then gently make a decision to train our minds. Everyone in prison feels pain, including both inmates and correctional staff. Suffering is a part of life. Facing pain dead on, while letting go of the thoughts that fuel it, creates a new wisdom. We come to know the concept of impermanence. Things are constantly changing. There is the birth of any given situation, followed by its death, as it is replaced by the next event of the moment.

Concentrating on the breath allows us a 360° view of life and death. We are in a place of observation. Coaching our minds, from this new perception, allows us to rise above the worlds of good and evil, the world of duality. We come to the place where we can say "this too shall pass." From this place, we can add compassion to what we clearly see, opening up our hearts to receive from the Universe what we need to deal with the present moment. We begin to develop intuition about our patterns of thoughts in reaction to the emotions we feel.

Twenty-three minutes of meditation is filling my head with thoughts of the past. I do my very best to come back to the breath; however, my mind is totally preoccupied. Meditation is teaching me not to judge these thoughts, only to observe them. I can see two distinct issues of thought feeding my churning emotions.

The first issue is the lack of compassion I have for myself. I can now understand how going over any past situation obsessively is not kind. In coming back to my breath, I am relinquishing my power over this thought, allowing the power greater than myself to heal me of this shortcoming. The second issue happens when I am engaged in compulsive thought throughout the day. I am absorbed in thinking about the past or the future and not being present for the current moment. Consequently, I lose things. I'm so preoccupied with what is going on in my head that I totally lose mindfulness of what is going on around me. I have a very long history of leaving things in places because I am not paying attention to the present moment. Today, I comprehend my inner fear is being fed by revisiting the past and trying to control the outcome of the future. Not being present has precipitated leaving things in various places.

Once I realize I have lost something, I continue to obsess on thoughts of the outcome of my search for that which was lost. I am sitting with this dilemma, not wishing to push it away. The key, for me, is to accept what is, while adding a small space provided by my consciousness of my breath to provide the necessary compassion to make better choices.

Today is the day to practice being present, so that I can deal more effectively with losing something. I have lost my water bottle. I don't know where I left it. Obsessing about trying to remember where I left it, berating myself for losing it, trying anxiously to control the outcome of finding it, are all thoughts in the past or the future. What comes to mind, in creating a pause through taking a deep breath, is a slogan I read, "Drive all blame into one." I accept that I have lost the item. I practice the mind-training slogan to be compassionate and kind to myself. I even practice being grateful for having the opportunity to have this time of being incarcerated to work on this issue. This is a new way of looking at the situation.

I make a decision to let go of the worry and not replay the incident over and over in my head. Continuing to obsess keeps me from being present. I could lose more things! I make a plan to buy a new water bottle and accept the cost. I am training my mind in new paths around painful events.

In buying a new bottle at the commissary, I agree to let go and let God. Almost a year later, the inmate in charge of the recreation office, also a member of the protestant church service I attend, stops me to ask me if the bottle he found with the word "Buddah" inscribed on it in black permanent marker is mine. Sure enough, it is. In practicing my refusal to blame, and in dealing with the loss, it seems the Universe has returned my bottle. Perhaps, it is in recognition of my hard work. Since I have another bottle, I celebrate my joy by giving the bottle away to someone who needs it. I gift it to someone who cannot not afford one, because he is new to the compound. I admit to myself that I am not cured of this issue by any means, yet I acknowledge the grace bestowed upon me in the present moment.

I am grateful for my breath. I can train my mind by associating my breath with many new and peaceful ways of acting toward painful and joyous events. I make progress in the process of change. I am on the path.

January 20th

Let's explore the phrase, "Let go and let God." Instead of conjuring up old thoughts and beliefs about the "G" word, we can start fresh in the present moment and make the choice to create a new expanded outlook.

When we become aware of our bodies, we can see how letting go of our emotions, once we are aware of them, relaxes us. When we add tender-loving-kindness, our physical relationship to the world becomes more serene. As we increase our cognizance of each part of our anatomy, we spend less time in the compulsive thoughts that feed our conflicting emotions. We let go of our worries by changing what we can through our concentration. We don't deny the emotion, we change our perspective to be with what troubles us.

We can face the continuous chatter in our minds with the increased scope of vastness and emptiness. Letting go of any thought, without labeling it good or bad, allows us to start any moment over, at any time. We can change any direction we're headed, such as storing up resentments, and drop the pebbles of discontent before they grow into boulders around our necks.

We can become more conscious of any feelings we have, owning FLAGSS (fear, loneliness, anger, guilt, shame and sadness) and letting go from the space we develop in our hearts. By doing so, we become more honest about owning our emotions 100%, while starting to replace the stress of control with the peace of compassion toward ourselves.

What we release is our ego's need to master an outcome. What we need to fill the void is our trust in a reborn faith and hope. We remain in the world, but we focus our vision in the realm of spiritual eternity. We come to know that everything physical has a beginning and an end. The ethereal brings up pure love. We are fulfilled from the inside, becoming a living conduit of being-ness that knows no end.

God is not externally defined, but experientially confirmed. Letting go is an action by which we can increase our familiarity with peace.

I finish my meditation and go off to work. During the day, I cough. Immediately someone said tersely, "Cover your cough." I am taken aback because I had covered my mouth with my fist. Then, I was "shown" how to cover my cough, being given the CDC method for covering a cough. My first reaction is not spiritual. I feel an immediate aversion to his comment. *"Who is he? My mother?"*

I give the situation space enough not to say what is going on in my mind. Rather, I explain that what I have (asthma) isn't catchy. The response I get is even more aggressive.

"I don't care. Cover your F…king cough!"

I immediately remove myself from the situation and go to one of my spiritual contacts to help me resolve the situation.

The ego part of me thinks, *"I'm not going to let anyone cuss me out-period!"* My teeth are clenched! I am definitely not happy. My goal is to get even and then set some sort of boundary.

I share my soul and the feedback I get resonates with my practice:

- Have a direct experience with the anger. I need to feel where it resides in my body.
- Move away from identifying with the duality of who is right and who is wrong. This is the world! Do not give my power away to another.
- The goal is to use my awareness to take action. I intend to take the upper hand in a way that brings peace.

I run into the person later and I apologize for my reaction causing harm. My intention was never to do so.

"My sincerest apology for my reaction," comes my attempt to create peace. What I get back is, "What kind of sarcastic response is that?" I continue, "I sincerely do not wish to cause any harm. I'm doing my best, and I promise you I am not sarcastic." To that, in the presence of another who encourages him, he says, "Okay! Then, he apologizes to me for using profanity, saying,

"Things just got out of hand." I bow and we go our own separate ways.

My first response is less than perfect; however, with the support of others here, that are working a spiritual program right along with me, I am able to let go of my ego and allow the God of my understanding to take control of the outcome. It is really fulfilling to have experienced resolution. I used the love that I needed from within, and shared outwardly.

Later in the day, I revisit the past, being quite judgmental from the position of my ego. Immediately, I realize what is happening and I move to the present moment. I remind myself that revisiting a past resentment is only going to ruin **me** - not the other person. Again, I let go and let GOD! I can now be open and spacious enough to be fully present with the moment in front of me.

January 21st

The intention of meditation is to spend time in silence so as to create the space necessary to be open to wisdom (within the spirit) and away from knowledge (within the mind). This wisdom is not predictable, nor can we crave it or control it into existence. We must become willing, in our practice, to be available to receive.

We move in a direction that makes progress, not perfection. Just a gap of quiet mind allows us to deepen our relationship with this space, to gently become aware of blaming either ourselves, or what's in front of us, as the culprit for our unhappiness. This momentary pause, taken over and over (by saying "thinking") helps us clean our side of the street with a double-edged sword. Clear seeing and the practice of compassion that starts within us first. This place in the middle cuts to the heart of the matter We fuel our practice by being willing to take a step toward creating steadfastness.

My practice brings me to see clearly the fear that comes with self-doubt. For me, the solution is simple. There is no self to fortify in silence. There is only the energy of fear to place at the altar of wisdom. Underneath any self-righteousness is this fear. Between the inward breath and the outward breath, I come to be available for wisdom to speak to me. It's random. I cannot pin it down. I cannot think it into existence. I use the three C's. I can't control it. I don't cause it. I can't cure myself of the dissatisfaction that comes with powerful, painful emotions.

In meditation I yield to the force greater than what my ego believes. I want a solution to all my problems. This thought has two errors: the emphasis on "I" and the craving of "want".

I intend to be willing to sit today. It's that simple. The power of wisdom does the rest. I come to believe in a power greater than myself that restores me to sanity (the 2nd step of any 12-step program). Saneness is always there. It's not lost. I just become aware of it. I am planting the seeds of compassion and kindness.

January 22nd

Continuing to see our lives as clearly as we can, while adding compassion to bring us toward a peaceful center, sets the stage for how we deal with speech. Speech is that which comes from others, and even more important as to weight, that which comes from within us.

Language used in an institutional setting (such as this) tends to be bitter. Adding our own speech to the mix further poisons the total experience; it solidifies a life that is off center. Staying away from judgment, we raise our level of consciousness around our use of speech. This is a huge undertaking. We can wisely admit that we will have failures in achieving the goal of uplifting speech. The solution is better reached if we see ourselves as connected to the whole. Speech affects everyone.

There's a verse to a song that comes to mind, bringing focus to the target of speech:

"Let peace* begin *with me, let this be the moment now…"

All we need do is continue our willingness past monitoring our thoughts, to being conscious of what words we use towards one another.

With the concept that we are all connected, we can now take on the compassion of forgiving the words of others that cause damage. We can't control the negativity, that devastates the air, when it comes out of someone else's mouth. This takes courage on our part. The path takes us to the middle ground. We can forgive aggression. We can face the pain. We can reduce our ignorance by becoming more conscious of what speech does in our lives.

I observe an inmate going to the C/O's office to ask for a writing tablet. The C/O tells the inmate he has paper. That's the answer to the first question. The inmate asks for a pad and the answer to the second question is "NO!" This starts the ball rolling and the speech used is pretty aggressive: c..k s..ker, m..f..ker, as.h.le. I see how the inmate responds to the C/O's sarcasm, yet I remain neutral.

The reactions of others are swift. The inmate is cuffed and taken off to the SHU. I continue doing my best not to judge, only to be present for the speech that was used and to wait for the wisdom, so I could learn from the situation.

I'm reminded that when I'm thinking, I just label it "thinking" and let go without judgment. I just breathe in the negativity from the C/O's answer and the inmate's reactive response. I breathe out compassion for myself first, then to both the C/O and the inmate. If we're all connected, then the fact that we're all in separate bodies is an illusion. So, I practice that. I go to the middle ground: not being aggressive, nor pushing away the pain I feel for everyone concerned, and I do my best to expand my level of consciousness to the big picture.

A year from now, I will read this passage and it will seem clearer. I processed this situation in the present moment and now it's no longer permanent. In fact, down the road a bit, this C/O will no longer supervise this unit. The inmate will be out of the SHU and back in a different room. Life will have moved on. I won't have stored up any unfinished resentments by doing my practice.

The wisdom I am gaining centers around practicing these principles in all of my affairs. I can then live an emotionally free life in here. Forgiveness for me, and others, keeps my side of the street clean.

January 23rd

Brick by brick, we begin adding to the foundation of a new way of life. Moving deeper into our practice, we become conscious of the difference between action and reaction. A moment of action comes from the space of being with the breath and is self-fulfilling. It needs no additions or subtractions because it just is. Reaction to any given situation from the moment comes from a place of want. It is co-dependent, out of balance, and creates a chain reaction of discursiveness to feed our discontent.

A life of action brings peace. We take our raw emotions along with us, opening our hearts and minds to what new wisdom may be bestowed upon us. The focus is not what could be learned; it is just being with our feelings, watching our thoughts as an observer, letting go and making decisions to turn our wills and our lives over to the care of a higher power. We act from a place of vastness. We also act from a place of emptiness. There is no preconceived notion as to what the outcome may be. We encounter a new steadfastness that anchors us further to life in the present moment.

I sit in the common area of the unit. I choose the smaller TV room because it is a place people come to watch the news. The larger TV room is filled with drama, so I avoid it to remain peaceful. I don't really need TV. I come to continue my practice, after my sitting meditation.

Near me, there is another man listening to his music. His ear buds are in both ears and he is wrapped up in his enjoyment. He's also having something to eat. Each piece of his treat is individually wrapped. As he peels each indulgence, he throws the wrapper on the floor near him. My thoughts immediately are drawn to judging this man.

I want him to stop littering. That's a reactive thought. I refocus my intention to grow spiritually. I let go of what I'm thinking before it becomes speech that harms. I just sit with my dissatisfaction. I create as much space as I can and that is my first action. I let him be with his music and his rare pleasure. I watch my emotions.

I am aware of my need to "fix" the situation. I like fixing! I like making the world a better place; however, this thought that the world is not already a better place, just as it is, makes my life a huge mess. I am in this institution because I craved fixing a man's life, taking control of the situation and letting my ego be in charge of the outcome. In trying to do well, the Universe placed me in here to face the turbulence I have within me. It has nothing to do with any crime committed. It has to do with my intention, my speech, and my reactions to my belief system of how I think things should be.

I continue to watch as he throws more paper on the floor. I'm concentrating on how this perceived imperfection is going to take me to a higher level of understanding. That's not the goal, so I let go of any thoughts again and I just sit with my breath as he moves his hands to his ears' delight.

After tossing his last wrapper, he gets up from the chair and goes out of the small TV room. The pile of paper wrappers is on the floor. I wait another moment until he is completely out of sight. Without judgment, I pick up the wrappers very peacefully and put them in the trash can near the door. I do this because I have the ability to do so - and the consciousness as well. I did not spend any time lecturing the man who dropped the paper. He's probably unconscious as to his behavior. Wasn't I unconscious when I went to "fix" the man who arranged the meeting that sent me to prison? I forgive this man for littering as an expression that I forgive myself for not acting in a more spiritual manner. I can do this now! I'm connected to the man who left the room through the feeling of compassion.

Another inmate sees me pick up the paper quietly and place it in the trash can. He turns to me and says, "You're a good man." I thank him. I picked up the paper because of my level of consciousness toward the community. I allowed his level of unconsciousness to come into my heart on my inward breath, and I acted compassionately on the outward breath. As a result, it changed the person who witnessed the action. All he saw was my non-judgmental attitude and my deed.

I did not fix the man who dropped the wrappers. I change what I can. I change my reaction into an action. Without my focus on any outcome, I gained the respect of the person watching me. I take the gratitude I feel and I share it with the unit on my outward breath. I'm taking my practice from the bed and trying it out in my life today.

January 24th

Just as checking the six points of taking our seat during meditation (seat, torso, legs, hands, sight, and mouth), we can use our consciousness of intention, speech, and action to create a new livelihood one present moment at a time. We move away from what our ego wants to what our higher selves have to offer, which is an ever expanding understanding of what we need as a connected society.

Creating a space in meditation allows us to open up to a new way of life one small step at a time. Our intention is not to have expectations. Our speech is something we merely observe during and after our center of meditation. We become the observer of our actions, to see where we are opening up and where we are closing down. Gradually, we start to make small changes in the way we contribute to life wherever we are. We move away from craving and become more generous to ourselves and to those around us.

Bo Lozoff, the founder of the Human Kindness Foundation, says something very simple that gives us an idea of how to be conscious of livelihood. He says, "Do your own time!" He wrote a book entitled, We're All Doing Time. It's not just those incarcerated who have dissatisfaction. Even those on the street suffer through discursive thinking, speaking in ways that create more pain, and reacting to others in a way that can turn into a host of dramatic fiascos.

Through taking our seat every day, increasing a minute of our practice on a daily basis (we've reached twenty-eight minutes today), we become guided by the larger picture that the space we create provides. Livelihood is focusing on being conscious long term. We move forward being with and contributing to life.

In addition to my job in food service, which I really enjoy most days, my livelihood, while here, is to create this book one day at a time. Some days I come up with several topics and have a couple of contiguous days to create, writing out of my meditation. Other times, I leave a single idea on a page and move on to the next day. I come back to an idea I wrote one year earlier and make more progress, opening up to allow the text to flow from the center of my practice.

In working my practice, it's important to me not to focus on the whole book. There are parts that are not written during the days I am practicing. Seeing life in the past or wondering what life would be like in the future, including the finishing of this book, does not increase my wisdom. The book comes as I perform the basics.

I have come to prison, but not because I committed some crime. I have come here because fear brought me. I like fixing people! That urge still exists. I'm very aware of it. Today, I'm writing this book to uncover the true inner me, beyond fear or self-doubt. On the outward breath, expanding my practice, I send out this text to anyone who wishes to read and work the practice with me. The focus is on me at first. I need to practice compassion, kindness, joy, and balance on the cushion here. Then, I give it away without expectation of outcomes.

January 25th

Our practice brings us closer to dealing with pain, not moving away. Yet, if we only strive to dive brutally into the fire, we'll only be burned up before we reach any kind of enlightenment. We must also practice with ease. It's a lot like Goldilocks and the three bears - not too hard, not too soft, and just right!

We sit in our practice to do our best, not doing too much or too little, with some particular idea in mind. We bring who we are, with all our faults and assets, while we act with faith - a willingness to face adversity for what it is with a compassion that arises without effort. We make friends with the darkest parts of ourselves. We change our perspective by opening to the larger truth that all of us have something to contribute to this life (no matter where we come from).

We don't know what's in store in the future. We cannot change what is in the past. It takes courage to live in the present moment, while being gentle with ourselves. This is living with balance. We sit on what the spiritual teachers call "the razor's edge". By actually practicing gentle steadfastness, we learn to eat the elephant of life one bite at a time - one thought, one feeling, and one moment.

I'm an overachiever. I am aware that I over do. These are thoughts that I leave on the breath. Taking more than my share of the responsibility for any situation is something I lay at the altar of the present moment. Doing too much comes from a place of deficit, where I want to control the outcome of any situation.

Instead, I purpose to sit with fear and self-doubt. On the other side of imbalance, I sit with self-righteousness. I breathe in the pain of being powerless over the craving to fix the world. I am aware that I'm the one who gets burned in the process. I take a step back today, giving space to my discomfort in not being able to control peaceful outcomes.

Instead, I am sitting with the horror of what has happened to my life and where I am today. It's not permanent. I am courageous in my practice. Off the cushion, I ask for help from those I have learned to trust over the years. I practice patience to let the uncertainty unfold gently. I work on this book, when I can, and on the days I'm blocked, I just sit and realize I'm stuck. And wait. I keep coming back to the breath to go one step further into faith, one stride toward being enough, just for today. I am reminded that I am not the only one facing this type of pain. Everyone faces emotional turmoil. I'm not alone! I take the position of becoming the watcher of my life, waiting to see what may come in the door in each present moment. I make a pledge to take today and take action on the task to be open to soft spiritual growth. I finish one more page of the book. It's for me, first and foremost. Then, I give it away unconditionally.

January 26th

Mindfulness is the process of filling up, being present in ways that anchor us further to the present moment. Being with the breath is the groundbreaking of constructing a temple within us. We can add being with all the parts of our bodies. We can go to the place within us where we feel emotions: fear, loneliness, anger, guilt, shame, and sadness.

If we get lost in thought, we can come back to the breath again and again. We practice letting go, emptying ourselves out. It's like pouring out a cup full of an old way of life, leaving nothing. If it fills back up with familiar habits, we must empty the cup over and over again. With that emptiness comes a vast array of wisdom that exists in the unmanifested. It's wisdom waiting to fill and pronounce who we are.

Silence and progressive awareness of being present for ourselves is mindfulness. We soak up vastness and emptiness. We don't try to define it. We just act. We don't think our way into the solution; we merely are with whatever we face now.

I go to the spiritual gym after lunch on Saturday. I don't speak to anyone. I go to my bed and practice. I listen to the sounds, letting go of judgment. I observe my body and my feelings. I fast, except for a cup of tea when I take a break.

I meditate for thirty minutes. I stretch. I feel how my body reacts to sitting. I do another thirty minutes. I gently bring myself back when I become lost in thought. It's just "thinking". It passes and I come back to my breath, my body, the fear I feel, and the hopelessness that arises. I let whatever I feel dissolve as I let go, emptying myself out, allowing a power greater than my ego to speak to me at any given moment. I am a human being, instead of a human doing.

I have come to realize that wisdom is random. It has no rhyme or reason. I just have to be open to receive it. To shut down means I could miss something important. That's a thought, so I let that go as well. By being in my spiritual gym, I am connected to the whole. My awareness strengthens my willingness to gently go to the space where compassion and kindness can be practiced.

I stop on Sunday to eat dinner and go to church.

January 27th

Now that we have all the general basics for meditation, a technique to practice living life from the inside out, rather than reacting from the outside in, our focus becomes being present for any element that comes into our lives. We create clearer seeing and compassion.

Whatever passes in front of us is the teacher and we are the students, to till and fertilize the soil of our souls. We can rise above the existence of suffering to a spiritual perspective of progressive expansion.

Today is the day of the perfect storm for my education. The lessons are endless. I am aware that it takes courage to face what I feel and the rewards of wisdom take me to a wider scope of understanding. It is a day for scholarship, to be <u>in</u> this world of prison, but not <u>of</u> it.

First snow, then fog, the compound is shut down all day for security reasons. Even all the food service workers are sent back to their units.

I go deeper into my practice on my bed. I sit with impatience, and breathe out compassion for myself, then for all those inmates on the compound. I go further. This isn't an easy day for the correctional staff either. They have to make today's meals and deliver them to us. I breathe in the pain on their side. I start with compassion for myself first, then to them. I'm learning that I stumble when I start with myself. That's not my first reaction. That's a thought, so I go back to sending the healing energy of compassion and tender-loving-kindness from the space within and then outward, all the way to the mountains.

I am present to hear all the emotional distress, yet I don't allow it to penetrate who I am. It's reactive speech, so I'm silent. It's not permanent. The fog will eventually lift. All sides of the compound are connected by all this pain caused, not by the weather, but by our reaction to the weather. I use the time to practice. I have the time. I'm not going anywhere. I'm reminded that creating resentment is like drinking poison and expecting the other person to die.

I take a shower and work on this book. All this practicing has been like doing a daily fire drill. Now that the fire has actually come, I'm aware of how to be, not what to do. I spend my time taking care of myself. I am clean. I've had something to eat, compliments of the correctional staff. I take a nap, setting my alarm to stand for count when it is needed.

There is a lot of discontent around me, yet I remain peaceful until I prepare for bed. I continue breathing in emotional pain as I hear it arise and I breathe out compassion. I'm aware that I am faking it, mostly. I'm honest about that. Compassion doesn't swell up inside me. I'm just learning to turn on the faucet. It is what it is. I'm gentle with my approach. That's new! I'm reminded not to beat myself over the head with the sages who reach out to me in all the books I read. "Thank you Pema Chodron, I'm listening to you."

The sun comes out the next day and life in prison goes back to normal. I have to laugh here. "What is normal?" I'm adding humor to my practice! It's not about pushing the pain away. I'm just watching it, creating some space to be with myself.

January 28th

From the space of balance come opportunities to be coached in patience. Grasping at what we want comes from believing that a person, place or thing will settle all our desires. That's a very narrow view of truth. It is an ego truth and that brings us back to pain and powerlessness.

If we concentrate on why we're impatient, we're looking at the object, instead of the impatient mind. Now, let's continue to go inward, deeper into the simple idea that the mind feeds impatience with thought. Let's just be with the impatient mind - letting go of the thoughts that fuel our irritation.

I grind my teeth when I'm impatient. Coming to grips with this awareness doesn't stop me. I quietly stop the motion and come to rest. Sooner or later, I start up again. Gently, I come back to the breath, instead of grinding my teeth. I am developing patience by looking directly at the feeling, instead of trying to control the gnashing of my teeth. That's one lesson for the day.

The line for pizza is slow. There is a very long wait. I'm learning to laugh at life here. Inmates CRAVE these little pizzas and there's so much theft, it jams the whole process. That's a thought, too, so I let that go and just sit with the energy of impatience. I am very impatient with myself. That's a thought that feeds grinding my teeth. I let that go and breathe out compassion for myself, while relaxing my jaw.

I practice compassion for those having to deal with the slow line. Again, it starts with me and then goes outward. I send out compassion to the correctional officers too. Pizza is like fried chicken, only it's harder to control this food because it comes out of the bakery. I keep a small daily meditation book with me at all times. I read from it, instead of concentrating on my hunger. Once I sit down, I watch the three "J's" go back in line for another piece. I watch my judgmental thoughts as they arise. I practice patience, letting go of the ruling. I practice my vow of non-attachment.

G is so annoyed that he didn't get a piece of pizza. He is so impatient, he leaves the dining hall and goes back to his room to fill himself with self-righteous indignation. I practice breathing in his pain, breathing out compassion. It's just pizza. I focus on the times when I lose patience and become self-righteous. That connects me to the whole. I'm in between the greed of gluttony and narcissism. I am practicing being satisfied with what's given.

I sit with all of this turmoil over a reaction to this little pizza. I get extra vegetables and I'm full. The truth is, I never go hungry here. There are always plenty of side dishes. So much food gets thrown away here. That's another thought. I sit with the feelings of sadness and let them go. Lunch is over!

The Buddha expressed the wisdom that we can turn arrows into flowers. I understand this proverb in a simple way. I have so many things to write about! I'm grateful for that. I'm turning bad situations into pages.

"When faced with lemons, make lemonade!"

January 29th

Our egos are shortsighted. This outside focus is narrow and often hypocritical. Seeing out is seeing the bigger picture. Instead of getting rid of the ego, we can be curious to the idea that we're all connected. If we do not understand the larger concept now, we can use this opportunity to experiment with creating a new way of life. We can ask the question, "Does unconditional love already exist within us, within our presence of being?" Creation, Love, and Being are all deeper levels of consciousness that we come to remember. It already exists deep within us. We've just forgotten them because of our narrow egoical view.

It's hard to see the bigger picture when we feel pain. The dissatisfaction of prison is filled with discordant opposites! To admit that we feel pain encourages us to take a step out of our comfort zone, outward and upward. This is a step toward spiritual awakening. We do not assume we will have a more panoramic view, which is an outside narrow view. Joy comes from within. We already have it. We just have to keep coming back to the breath to be open to see it as it is. We become aware of how joy deepens on its own.

An inmate is angry at me, because last month he was paid full-time by accident, and this month his time was adjusted, by the staff accountant, to balance his account. He wants to blame me! I can't change his reaction. I'm only the main clerk. There is a mistake causing this man pain. I'm facing the pain of his disapproval. The staff accountant made the mistake. The larger perspective is, I can't really judge her either. After all, didn't I make an error in judgment that landed me in here? I'm worth being forgiven. The accountant is worth being forgiven. The inmate in front of me is worth being forgiven. Bad things just happen.

On the other side of my day, my mind reminds me that my co-worker does very little, compared to the amount of work I do; yet, he gets paid the maximum (the same as I do). I have to surrender to the larger perspective and lead by example. I have to rise above a second scenario that could lead to blame. This takes tremendous courage on my part.

Clear-seeing lets me know that bad things do happen. People do get paid for work they don't do. I can only take responsibility for myself. A wise man (the author of Desiderata) reminds me not to compare myself to others. It would lead to becoming bitter and vain.

Compassion is calling on the space to fill me with the wisdom that I work hard for all of us. I can take comfort that I have a great work ethic. I'm writing this book to keep me on track while I'm here. And yet, I feel as though even the book is for all of us. The compassionate view, for me, is not to overdo it. All of this will pass. (As I am typing this manuscript, I see that all has indeed passed. Yet, I still have to practice these principles in the present moment.)

January 30th

All solutions to living are successfully achieved by going inside ourselves. Here is where we start with an awareness of our current state of consciousness. We make friends with this level and start where we are.

20th Century Psychology describes the root of all addictions to codependency and the lack of inward consciousness. Keeping it simple, we sit in meditation to exercise our conscious understanding, while moving toward a peaceful conclusion to all matters.

Once we realize our codependent minds are the managers of our reactions, we can start to develop a curious compassionate friendship with whatever state we find.

If we're the most resentful, fearful, self-righteous individual in our unit, we start with that. We accept where we are. We just make a decision to turn our focus from listening to our narrowly focused minds, to replacing it by paying attention to the outward breath. Our intention is not to grasp at the idea of living a life full of joy, but to be present to what is. Setting a goal to be the kindest, most peaceful inmate on the compound is focusing on an external outcome. Again, the focus is on the moment of now and where we are at that moment. We continue to practice looking clearly at what is, while adding whatever compassion and kindness we have available at the time.

I work with the distractions of my mind. I become aware that it doesn't take long before my mind wanders away, either talking to me about the past, or even more about what will happen in the future. I have constructed a list of character defects and taped it to the side of the locker by my bed. Number Four is discursive thought.

I am using mediation to make friends with my discursive mind. I am either craving something, trying to get away from something painful, or I'm not even conscious of some key awareness that will free me. This is where I am. Today, in being kind to myself, while training in clearer seeing, I keep coming back to my breath and the sound of my heartbeat. If I'm distracted by a sound in the unit, or my wandering mind, I just say "thinking" and come back to the beat and the outward breath.

I sit on a pillow, on the bed, as I practice. Not everyone has a pillow. I am aware of that. Without coveting it, or trying to use it to move me away from anything painful, I'm just aware that I am sitting on it while breathing, while my heart beats.

After meditation, I write something that comes to my mind. It goes like this:

- I met a man who was angry that he had no shoes, until he met a man that had no feet.

Meditation is my feet. I have this technique and I am dedicated to my practice. No matter what happens in here, I just do it with a sense of gentleness, when I can.

January 31st

Increasing our consciousness through meditation on a daily basis is the code for spiritual awakening. All three concepts (meditation, consciousness, and spiritual awakening) are built into the fabrication of all Twelve-Step Programs, starting with Alcoholics Anonymous, which was formed in 1939. We can begin to see ourselves more honestly. The direction of the journey is to see outward, away from the selfish ego called the addict.

In quiet contemplation we experience living in this world through a physical body; however, our search is to "be," which is not of this world. Simply put, we all just are! Every living creature has a living force. This energy connects us all as one balanced body. Each decision we make changes that balance.

One of the goals of reflection is to see beyond the self to the cumulative connective domain. Each day, we practice we start anew. We are freshly charged with what we gain from the empty space. There is nothing measurable to gain, as wisdom is not spiritual covetousness. The pause alone gives us a chance to turn away from any reaction - to make a choice that turns our wills over to the power greater than ourselves. This is the basic idea in Step Three of any Twelve Step Program.

J., a line server in the dining hall, accidentally rubs his nose with his gloved hand to alleviate an itch. Instead of reacting to the comment coming from the inmate across the line, "What the f..k you doin'? Wipe yer snot on yer glove, then handin' me the tray?

You do it again, I'm gonna whoop yer f..kin ass!", he just remains silent.

I am aware that his pause brings the following wisdom:

- The line has to continue to move. Each moment is impermanent.
- Meeting the inmate with an argument is a reaction that doesn't work. It's an outward solution to an inward problem.
- It is not the object of the discursive mind that is the problem; it is the discursive mind that needs the gentle focus.

The inmate leaves. The problem is resolved. The meal ends.

Wow! There is peace in silence.

February 1st

Let's bring the idea of failure into our practice. We've all failed at something that led us into this place. Meditation allows us to look at the higher purpose for failure. We don't just give up. We bring the feelings of hopelessness, shame, and guilt to the cushion; we sit to find our way to humility.

If we all are truly connected, no one is better than anyone else. Failure can be the seed that blossoms into something that changes the world. The choice is ours.

The spiritual perspective on worldly failure depends on what choices we make now. We start by helping ourselves. Once our cup is filled up, the humility we learn can be given away to others. We face the pain head on, developing a faith in a higher purpose that connects us. We let go of any outcome.

I am aware of the amount of time I spend going over the day of my arrest. I know what was on my mind. I know my intention for that day. Discursively, I think of all the many ways that would have better conveyed the truth; however, none of that soothes me. I cannot change the past. I practice not looking at my mind's discursiveness, but instead, at the failure of not being able to convey a message. I sit with the shame I feel over a story I told many years ago. Failure brings me to great sadness. I'm sad the world does not understand the truth; only I do. That's a thought, so I drop it and sit with the sadness.

The seeds of this writing come from the pain I feel. My practice comes from admitting my powerless over what the world "thinks" is the truth. Other people's opinions of me are none of my business. I can turn self-doubt into the seed that stabilizes my mind. I can take self-righteousness and use this failure to humble me to the point where I am equal to every other human being on earth.

In this practice, I am going into the space, opening up to the idea that everyone has a perfect higher self that deserves love. Everyone!! I open myself up to feeling compassion. I surrender to the possibility of tender-loving-kindness. I have failed, but I am not a failure.

February 2nd

We live our whole lives using our five senses - sight, hearing, touch, smell, and taste. Our thinking about what we sense keeps us locked into experiencing life in the physical sense; however, using the sixth sense, the ability to be conscious of what we do from the viewpoint of who we are, adds the dimension of wisdom to our lives over the knowledge gained through our base mind.

We practice meditation to distill our ability to quiet our mind and bring it to our presence. Spiritual acquisition is not the goal; such an ambition is not obtainable. We follow the path by seeing what is. What happens is an expanded vision arising in the present moment. Christians call this being reborn, becoming the truth of Christ's life example. Let's be open to the possibility that living in the present moment is what allowed Jesus to be free from sin. Going eastward, this is the same refined introspection exemplified by the practice of the Buddha (the enlightened one).

This soul searching is the foundation for mindfulness-observing our thoughts, emotions, our body sensations, the breath, and ultimately our faculty to let go of outcomes as a more wide open response to grief.

I am incarcerated today. Things could be a lot worse. There is no cell door. I live in a cubicle. I can come and go in the unit as I need to, except during a count, of course. I have the space and the time to practice sitting with my breath as often as I choose.

I can still see, hear, touch, smell, and taste. I have glasses to help me see. My practice helps me to gently stop reacting to the things I see that don't meet my mind's expectation of perfection. My hearing is still pretty good. Being aware of sounds with my breath allows me to see that sound has a beginning and an end. No sound goes on forever. The moments of silence that happen in my practice are the seeds of a new way of being. There are good smells and bad smells. They, too, come and go. I don't push bad smells away; I just sit with them until they pass. I have the opportunity to taste when I eat. I am never hungry. I'm grateful to taste an apple most every day. That's a simple gift. When I exercise, I move better. I feel better. I get to sit with my body, becoming more aware of how to be gentler with myself throughout the day. Finally, for the first time in my life, I am aware of my breath, not just on the meditation pillow. I catch being aware of my breath all throughout the day. I am realizing that, whether I am in prison or I am on the street, I have all my five senses and my ability to be conscious. I can use these anchors to bring me to now. Now is not dependent on where I am. It is being aware of who I am. I have become aware of my higher self.

February 3rd

When do we practice? The answer is simple. When it's most practical. When is there less noise to get started? Perhaps we can wake up early enough where the morning is quiet enough to start our practice. If that doesn't work we can choose a time, after the last count of the evening, after everyone has settled down for the night. The key is to be gentle with ourselves, while seeing more clearly. Everything we do in our practice comes from two points toward the middle ground. We live in a word of duality. Our mission is to work with it.

We also have to take into account what kind of job we have and what times we have to go to work. There might be time during our days work that we're not doing anything at all. What a perfect time to practice. In the beginning, we don't try and practice when it's loud and there's a lot of movement. We're just getting started. Tenderness must accompany uncovering the obvious. Peace isn't right or wrong, it just is!

I find the period just after midnight is a great time for me to sit and practice. There is an overwhelming existence of silence, even with the snoring in the darkness. Very few people move during this time of day. I am conscious when the C/O's come by with their flashlights to do the last count of the night. *"What if they judge me for my practice?"* That's a thought and I come back to my breath.

I work in the afternoon now, so this is a perfect time for me. I sit comfortably on my pillow, positioned on my mattress. The faint lights on the unit create a gray haze. It takes courage to do this! I seem to be the only person in my unit to work with this practice. That, too, is a thought, so I go back to my breath again.

I can hear my heartbeat because it is so quiet. When I am still, I can feel the pulses throughout my body. I add something to my practice tonight. I call it a mantra. When I breathe out I say "I". When I breathe in I say "AM". On the inward breath I let go. The spirit part of me is vast and empty- indefinable. Coming back to the outward breath, I have an awareness that keeps me focused. If I wander away, I just come back on the outgoing breath, (saying "thinking") while being present for my body, my breath, and any emotions that arrive.

After my 38 minutes, I lie down and continue the mantra until I fall asleep.

*Note: After a year of this practice, the C/O's start calling me Buddha. I am humbled by the respect that I receive from many who supervise the unit. I don't come to crave or expect the esteem; however, I bring it to my practice. I send out the kindness I receive from them. I send it out on my outward breath as far as I can expand in any given day's practice.

February 4th

Making friends with our thoughts is worth our attention. Obsessive dialogue within creates emotional intensity, or procrastination and negligence. The focus is inward, so we have the opportunity to observe only what our thinking is doing to cloud our minds. In Christianity, this is called sin. Because this word is so overused and abused, let's take a fresh approach to the fundamental idea of missing the mark (the loosely translated meaning from the original language).

Our compulsive thinking brings us to miss the mark, instead of processing and letting go of negative feelings such as fear, loneliness, anger, guilt, shame, and sadness. Meditation allows us to be present with our thoughts, making them our friends by saying "thinking" aloud, then being clear enough to turn our attention to our breath. We can begin to see thoughts as impermanent and not all that solid. Moment by moment, even intense emotional energy can be resolved.

Just practicing meditation sets us up to turn away from our compulsive lack of consciousness; we repent - another overused Christian word. Again, let's use a light, airy approach and endorse the idea of repentance as thinking again, a reflection that has a broader, wiser essence. The larger perspective leads us to hit the mark. We can experience our feelings with our feet firmly planted in the space until the energy passes. This new expression of faith has no goal. There is only the path.

I am making friends with my compulsive mind. The sages tell me not to beat myself up for getting carried away in my ego's reflection. Chogyam Trungpa Rinpoche and Pema Chodron both speak of "touching thoughts with a feather", then letting them go. These thoughts are making me very unhappy. Secondly, my egoic mind is manufacturing this unhappiness. That's a simple theory to become gently curious about.

The solution, then, is to turn away and let go, to go back to the vast empty space of my breath. I am making progress just by taking my seat today. There is no goal to be thought free! That's taking a beating to my training. Making a commitment to come to the meditation fitness center today is the fourth dimension of my practice. I am putting my confidence and trust in the space of unconditional love. The energy arises randomly. I bring all my painful, raw feelings and dump them into the gap of silence. I watch the situation at hand. I ask my great sadness to sit with me, right here on the bed. I am not the only person feeling this way right now. There is a whole compound full of sadness, emanating from the correctional officers, staff members and inmates. We're all connected on this compound. There is no "us vs. them." Sadness just is. I re-pent (go higher than the level of thinking to where the place of wisdom exists) and bring the wailing of my soul to the arms of compassion. I find myself grabbing a blanket and wrapping it around my body in the dark. This too shall pass!

Prayer: GOD, I love you with all my heart. You are inside me. Forgive me and forgive us all. I am committed to facing my pain and dropping it with a faith and a hope. I'm not asking you to take away my dissatisfaction, only to help me to make better decisions based on your wisdom. I turn my will over to your care. It's the first time I've realized we all deserve unconditional love. I'm no different. I open my heart and let go! Good night!

February 5th

Today, we have reached our meditation goal of forty minutes! Let's explore the phrase "I want" more deeply today. This need to control outcomes, to have our way, and to be self-absorbed is called narcissism. It abounds in prison. We use narcissistic behavior to try and make the pain go away, but it only removes us further from who we really are. Meditation, the means to clarify all present moments with wisdom, brings us to the understanding that "I","ME" and "MINE" are all illusions that bring great anguish. Selfishness is a corrupted attempt to solve the wrong problem from the wrong end. The wisdom of the present moment helps us to focus on the process, not the outcome. This is an inward process, not outward grasping.

Underneath the drive of self-centered behavior is the desire to appease what our culture defines as "negative emotions". We desperately want negative emotion to go away. We want to end the suffering caused by strong feelings such as fear, loneliness, anger, guilt, shame, sadness, abandonment…. and the list goes on and on.

What happens when we stop the discursive thoughts that feed these emotions? Let's experiment with the phrase "I Have". Perhaps creating a gap of silence will help us to change directions, allowing the wisdom of "I have" to arise. This is an attitude of gratitude. We do two things when we focus on what we have, what we're truly grateful for, instead of what we want.

1) We begin to see clearly that strong emotions, which we reflexively move away from, are worth moving towards. We make these painful emotions our friends. We invite them into the space we create.

2) We begin to become more compassionate with ourselves and, through opening up, we come to realize our connection to others. We start to share, instead of take,

through our awareness. We see that all of us face these emotions. There is no "I" to be selfish about. Compassion is always there; we have it. We already have the capacity of being fulfilled.

It's fried chicken day and the masses are alive with how many pieces they want. How many pieces can we shove into our jock straps and carry out of the dining hall?

- We take more than we need and we sell it.
- Some of us overeat, if we can arrange it.
- We create intensity around the event to cover up the need to be responsible for the emotion of anger.

These are all thoughts. I let them go in the silence of my meditation. I practice right in the dining hall. I breathe in all the anger and the greed, all the "want" that exists. I breathe out compassion for myself first, and then I extend it slowly to those I see. I am content with what I have to eat in front of me. I eat it as much in the moment as I can today.

The key, for me, is not to judge others. I "want" them to act a specific way, just like I want the chicken. I'm no different. I'm just using a different object to want. It's not what they're doing that's the problem at all. It's how I think about it. I go back to the breath and continue to express compassion for all the anger and sadness that occurs during this fried chicken meal.

I'm aware of my own selfishness. That is all I need to focus right now. I'm learning to lean into my own pain and make it my friend. I am practicing an attitude of gratitude.

February 6th

When I sit still, one wisdom which may arise is the concept of relativity. In other words, how we perceive any instance depends on what we have experienced in the past. We judge things based on where we are in the world of duality. Black is relatively dark to gray; however gray is relatively dark to white. So, what is gray? When it's paired with black, it's lighter; however, when it's paired with white it's darker. When it all boils down, or shall we say when our comprehension moves above the necessity for measurement, we can see clearly and let go of the dual perspective in favor of the absolute in the spiritual realm. Black just is. Gray just is. White just is!

We are learning to allow The Universe to speak for itself, instead of drawing our own conclusions. From a scientific point of view, meditation reshapes our brains. Many years ago, it was thought that one could not change one's brain at all. Now, relative to new discoveries, we're finding out the brain can change. Meditation has brought a new flexibility. Things are not cast in stone, as once believed. We can learn to face problems in a new way:

1) **We don't draw a target conclusion.**

2) **We go from the mind to the heart.**

3) **We begin to see each teachable moment to wake up.**

4) **We start seeing moments as impermanent, while the spirit of consciousness is eternal.**

Today is hamburger day. There is something left over at the end of lunch. A whole group of inmates are hovering around to get their fill. This reminds me of flies hovering around a dump of waste.

Here, I choose to watch how I react to the situation. Instead of circular thinking, focused around either the past or the future rumination, I'm choosing to watch my breath. I'm anchoring to the present moment. Rather than focusing on what will happen to the hamburgers, or the people who want the hamburgers, or whether or not I can have an extra hamburger, or my need to do the right thing by not wanting an extra hamburger, I choose to see this whole scenario as something impermanent. It's happening now and this too shall pass.

February 7th

Meditation brings sanity because it allows us to reach towards the vast emptiness above the physical world through presence. We submit our full participation with all our six avenues of familiarity - sight, sound, smell, touch, taste, and add the mindfulness of consciousness.

There is a relationship between consciousness and the physical. The spiritual cannot exist without the physical and the physical cannot exist without the spiritual. There is a phrase that makes it simple: form is emptiness and emptiness is form. Whether it's the alpha and the omega (the beginning and the end) or ying/yang, there is no separation. It's like trying to solve the problem of which came first - the chicken or the egg. I AM just is. There is birth, and then there is death.

"I" is not solid and is interrelated to every existing thing. All are bound by consciousness (AM). We come to the meditation cushion to observe and accept obsessive compulsive thought as a practice. We don't push thoughts away. We make a direct acquaintance with them without grabbing hold of them. We gently peel back the thought and let it go to experience the feeling state underneath, without being moved off our balance.

Thoughts are not permanent. Owning such thoughts is the root of our dissatisfaction. We take the thoughts as personal. This practice is about not taking anything personally. We just watch what rolls into our mind and watch those thoughts dissolve.

Today. I focus on an image within my mind to emphasize that all time is impermanent. I'm sitting in a field. It is a bright, sunny day with only a few clouds. I have a magnifying glass, a piece of paper and a glass of water. I sit, check my posture (seat, legs, torso, hands, eyes, mouth), and place the magnifying glass over the paper.

As I focus the magnifying glass over the paper, the sun becomes a very small point. A cloud moves past and the sun disappears for a while. This is thought. I observe it with clear seeing and gentleness, say "thinking" and wait for it to pass. The sun comes out again, and I refocus my magnifying glass until the sun comes to a point. The paper then begins to smoke and burn. I watch as the sun consumes the paper in fire. I lift the glass of water and pour it over the flames and then go back to my breath.

The magnifying glass is my practice. The sun is the vast emptiness from which all wisdom comes. The paper is my ego. I falsely identify with my ego and make all life experiences personal. The clouds are distractions of thought that come and go. If I sharpen my practice and allow moments of silence to coexist with my breath, the vast emptiness goes to the root of the emotion I am experiencing. The emotional energy, combined with the energy of the sun, burn away my ego until there is only ash. With gentleness, I pour the water over the paper as compassion and tender-loving-kindness. My breath is always there. All I have to do is come back to it.

I spend the rest of my session clearly being with my outward breath, letting go of any cloud that comes in my stream of consciousness.

I often learn a lot about myself from watching others. D. takes three pieces of cake [intending on giving two to other people]. I watch as observers come to project, “You got enough cake there?” The sarcasm is pretty strong. In actuality, D takes one piece for himself and gives one piece to K and one piece to G.

I am becoming aware of how my mind makes assumptions without asking questions. This takes focus in the now.

There’s a Buddhist Slogan that says, “Let the world speak for itself.” The power of now gives me the opportunity to pause and give space to allow things to unfold, before I start making guesses about what I believe is going on. In the long run, it’s none of my business how many pieces of cake someone takes, to widen the truth.

The Sun= Energy of The Universe

Magnifying glass= Practicing meditation

Moving the magnifying glass= Focusing on the breath

Paper= My body, senses, feeling states/thoughts

February 8th

With every day that passes, something inevitably goes wrong within any given moment. The natural human response is to take hold of pleasure and to move away from the pain.

Through practicing meditation, we begin to look at any given instance, whether pleasurable or agonizing, and question the highest truths:

1) **If each moment is separate in terms of our experience, is any event in a moment lasting or impermanent?**

2) **Is the person, place, or thing causing uneasiness, in any moment, able to sustain this hurtful episode?**

3) **Does identifying with the trouble ease or increase with our involvement? And even more empirical, with whom is this supposedly permanent self having this experience?**

A single answer repeatedly comes from meditation: everything is impermanent. We often react to persons, places, and things, but nothing is everlasting. Identifying with the permanent self escalates pain. In the spiritual realm, we are all connected with whatever we encounter.

Coming back to my breath, in the present moment, represents being inquisitive about the highest truth. I see that my ego wants to hold onto and solve every single, painful moment that comes across my path. Focusing on my breath allows me to live in each separate experiential moment. All of the thoughts I have about people, places, or things that create uneasiness within me just arise. Making the decision to come back to the breath allows me to let go of any sustainable reaction. This too shall pass.

My ego is not going to miraculously dissolve. I am learning to watch it with as clear an inventory as is possible in any given moment, while being gentle and kind to myself. This dual solution, dealing with the duality of the world of form, allows me to go to the middle ground that exists in the silence that arises. This small pause allows me the patience I need to act out the best possible decision now.

I experience a great deal of pain here. Holding onto it, by churning out thoughts, is not going to lead me to truth. As I meditate, I am learning to practice, in daily life, what I am doing on the cushion. I am sporadically watching as the haze of ache rises when I react to someone, something, or some place that offends the illusions of my ego. I am committed to my practice, not just for me, but for anyone who picks up this book to conduct this experiment with me.

February 9th

No one in prison likes being told what to do. The reaction is often anger; however, instead of looking at the two dimensional picture of who is wrong and who is right, the mindful meditation panorama moves us toward wisdom, rather than knowledge.

Knowledge is cut and dried, black or white. It is judgment, relying on established societal facts and norms. Wisdom, on the other hand, relies on going to the space of quiet, trusting in first hand experience as the guiding factor for making decisions. An inmate or a correctional officer can be unconscious. To judge them as right or wrong is a state of ego, of knowledge. Consciousness observes the behavior of others without judgment.

We don't accept what is handed to us, but instead, we give what is before us a mindful focus to come to believe in the highest truth. Wisdom connects us, where knowledge may separate us.

This wisdom we seek can be found inside the practice of observing and pausing. We undergo a transformation to acceptance through our willingness to open our hearts to first-hand instruction. The relationship with an unconscious person, through meditation, switches from what is true or false, to what is observed. Once we are clear that another's mental state is unconscious, we see trying to change them, or dispute them, makes us just as unconscious. What people do changes from moment to moment. Who they are is never to be judged as right or wrong. Unconsciousness confuses who we are with what we do. The key is to be present and remain neutral.

The warehouse man asks me to type up a few pages of things he needs to give to the food service director. He slides the papers under the door and I start to type what he has written.

After finishing, I slide both the written and typed pages back under the door. After a short while, the warehouse man comes to the window to tell me that what I typed was wrong. He starts to rant and rave, pointing at the pages. I listen. My ego wants to show I am right and he is wrong. I only typed what he wrote on the page.

I take a breath, just as in my practice and gently move myself above judgment of his actions, in an effort to be aware of what needs to be done in the present moment. I ask him to clarify, in writing, what he is saying. He writes down some notes on the page. I'm practicing not taking all this personally. I am staying away from who is right and who is wrong, only to clarify what needs to be retyped.

The pages come under the door and I retype them with the notes he has given me. I slide them back after I have finished. I let go. My ego wants a thank you. That's another judgment. It's thought and I let go. He comes to get the papers, looks them over, and goes back to work. Nothing is said.

My experiment with not judging brings me to see the opportunity to practice, in real life, what I do on the cushion. I am looking at a more conscious peaceful perspective. The project is complete. There is no blame. What I did, through wisdom, was to ask questions to clarify what he needed. Now, I go on to the next task on my desk.

February 10th

There is a wise saying which asserts that performing any activity continuously for more than thirty days can move that activity into a habit status. Meditation teaches us that life is a verb, not a noun, and an action worthy of a practice of custom.

In our choice to pause, life becomes an activity where boundless joy may arise. We experience a sense of gratitude. We begin to see that happiness occurs when we exist within the logic of genuine acceptance of what is. Finally, we make life meaningful by achieving efforts of generosity, compassion, and kindness.

Through a clear-seeing inventory of ourselves (from the inside out), surrounding ourselves with compassion, we come to value everything around us as equal. Good is something to enjoy and give away. Bad is an opportunity to stay grounded, adding our goodwill, until it passes. We all have character flaws and assets worthy of introspection. Our focus becomes our increased awareness of our thoughts, words and deeds as to how they affect the whole.

With a life of balance, we work on ourselves, because it is the sole driving force for selflessness. Ego is an illusion, as everything we do affects the whole. Understanding this habit of truth brings us to enjoy boundless happiness meaningfully.

I am aware that I'm practicing how to live a life of unconditional love, even though currently, I'm nowhere near that ideal. That's a thought that I'll let go. I am creating a life that recognizes everything as holy.

The habit of opening up just a bit more and allowing whatever enters my life to go directly to my heart, instead of regurgitating it in my mind, is the core of my practice. I give my practice forty minutes. I can break it up into two different sessions, if I wish. This is my personal spiritual vitamin that I am choosing to take each day.

I am developing a sense of what is not material. I spend each day strengthening my use of compassion, tender-loving-kindness, joyful exertion and equanimity, no matter what walks into my practice. Everything is an opportunity to grow.

During the day, I start to catch myself lost in mind chatter. I take a breath and restart at any given moment. I am open to Universal love and wisdom working through me, not around me, as before I came to this place.

February 11th

If sitting in meditation brings us to wisdom, while striving to reach a thorough state of spiritual perfection, it can also bring forth the consciousness of when ignorance is permeating our lives. This ignorant state can come in two forms – either by encountering something to which we've never been exposed or by a mal-practiced character defect we've incorrectly calculated as our truth.

When we probe deeper, whether it is our ignorant reaction to an unforeseen worldly event or it was gained through our own personality flaws, there lies a feeling state with which we can sit. In a state of reflection we can evaluate what we've done with what is reality.

At the moment we can admit that we're entirely ready to give up our imperfections to the space of meditation, we set into motion the assets of faith, hope and love. Now it is up to The Universe to reveal how truly flawed we really are.

Self-doubt is my number one character flaw. I see it clearly! Even when I "think" I'm right, I also see I allow someone else to sway me into doubting what is in my heart. This is what landed me here in this place. The fear of self-doubting is crushing!

The answer is to ask for help. I'm learning to ask others I trust for their input into an action plan that keeps me from committing emotional self-abuse. I recognize that asking for help allows me to open up, instead of choosing isolation. I'm ready to put this defect on the chopping block. I'm letting it go!

February 12th

Viewing the balance of the mind in meditation through the guidelines for the creation, listening to, and performing of music, we explore adding this as an object of focus. Just as the mind starts at rest and emptiness, so music starts with the staff (treble or bass). Then the tonic presents itself. This is the key of the music.

To find equilibrium, we keep coming back to the point of rest. In musical arrangements the wisdom of music always begins with the tonic and ends with a particular note. Then, the music resolves back to silence. The musical piece resembles our meditative practice. There are rests of silence amidst the scores of notes and words, trying to inspire us to a higher spiritual understanding.

Participating in the church choir brings me to music meditation. For me, this part of prison life comes closest to life on the outside. Everything seems to disappear, during rehearsal, as I learn, practice, and bring a new piece to fruition with the other members of the choir.

During church, when I sing, I've noticed it distinctly adds to the message. I am also conscious of a vague, particular awareness that comes from bringing together an ensemble of men who come from so many different faiths. The focus is the music and the message and how it affects my practice. I see the strife, a congregation of so many parts, some of it very harsh sounding. I practice opening my heart up to it. I face pain with music. I don't try to make the pain go away while singing. I come to the present moment of discontent, transcended by the flow of the emotional music.

A year and a half after my release, I come to a piece of music that cuts a hole through my heart. I bring all my senses to what is playing. The song is titled, *Hold On (The Secret Garden).* I see the notes dancing on the page, as I hear the music and the message. I can smell, while I taste its meaning, with my spiritual palette. I feel the beat on my skin and the wisdom of the words, all combining to bring me to tears.

February 13th

When we give our willingness to our sitting practice, what we experience is how to remain in the power of NOW (a phrase coined well by Eckhart Tolle in The Power of NOW) - the present moment. As we become more conscious, thoughts of the future or the past only feed emotional disturbance, because we can change neither. In the presence of now, we develop the courage to change the things we can.

What develops next is our awareness of cause and effect in succession. A classic example is the fact that the sun always rises in the east and sets in the west, never any other way - except on the occasion of a solar eclipse. However, what meditation brings to our attention is what we project is happening, based on what we see, hear, smell, taste and feel. We assume a lot when our prediction (what we believe) is most often dead wrong.

Instead of pushing away these unwanted projections or beliefs, we treat them the same way we contemplate ruminations of the past and the future. We allow them to rise and fall like the tides.

What is of greater importance is becoming more alert as to the way our emotions affect what we believe is reality. We can either be dulled to all that exists, run away from what is, or be thrown full throttle into a conclusion based on passion.

These feelings states are fed by compulsive thoughts and expectations that may or may not be true. The emotional pull within our minds may be compared to the static that occurs as we fine tune a radio to get the best reception of a certain station. I see this as ultimate truth.

Moving toward pain with a curious mind, while moving away from pleasure, allows us to increase the depths of our understanding and our reactive patterns. Without the objects

of our feelings as a focus, we can practice watching the energy of the emotion as it rises and falls.

D. does something nice for two people today. In the present moment, I am grateful to watch such kindness. My mind says, "*That* kind *of behavior is rare*." And that's a thought. I say thinking and live in the next moment.

I'm finding it takes courage to concentrate on the now when injustice occurs. I blow it all out of proportion with my compulsive thinking about the past! My ego goes into full swing. I see how I'm not staying in the now. My mind wants to create a story where I win.

Over and over, it's important to stop, be gentle with myself, and kindly go back to feeling my feet on the floor, notice a color in the room, sense my breath going in and out of my body. This storyline is not helping me. Leaning into pain without compulsive thought is really challenging!

This is only my path, not a destination. Leaning into pain without a storyline is also, still, a new habit to create. When I find myself being carried away in mindless chatter, I have the opportunity to be with the feeling states I'm experiencing. Even if I'm only a tiny bit successful in coming back to the present moment of now, it's a start.

February 14th

Action that reflects being brings balance. This is equanimity - the middle way. Here clear-seeing meets compassion, where natural joy arises. From this place of focus, we can observe the energy that comes up; we use this as a process, continuously coming back to the stillness of being.

In this place, things hidden become obvious for the first time, perhaps. Any situation can now come to a more vigilant space, even our stumbling blocks.

The closest we can come to who we are is by coming to our breath. This is the essence of our consciousness. Whether we believe we continue on past death is irrelevant. What matters most is the moment of now, that exists in each and every inhalation and exhalation. No matter our religious beliefs or our current spiritual understanding, everything starts with the breath of life.

In the midst of hungering for delight and avoiding discomfort, coming to the center of who we are, on the breath, brings us to the process of peace. In this place of harmony we find balance. In this place of balance we find peace.

Today, meditation is difficult! I'm in pain. I am committed to allowing any type of discursive thought with the emotional energy of grief. I see how heavy it is. I also see that my natural reaction to be kind and compassionate to myself does not flow naturally. I have used many things to make pain go away. Focusing away from the object of my discontent, just sitting with the ache of disappointment and hopelessness, I expand my horizon to just be. I share that with every living thing.

Instead of focusing on me, I do my best to be aware, on my breath, of all the people in the world who do not reflexively feel compassion and kindness for themselves. I am connected by this principle. My ego wants to blame mostly myself, yet in the now, I've not done anything wrong. I am practicing as best I can. I am living in the middle, between the inmates and the correctional officers, the middle way. Thinking about the past or the future makes things worse for me. It's all just conjecture. I keep coming back to my breath.

February 15th

As we come to the end of the foundation for practicing the process of meditation, let's look at the hypothesis that focuses on consciousness of the breath, the body, thoughts, and feelings which allows the brain the perfect scenario for learning faith, hope, love and being.

The scientific experiment to see if this hypothesis is true is "personally experiential." Only the individual can evaluate the wisdom of this theory. This is where science and the ethereal meet. This is the marriage of quantum physics and the bride of the steadfast church. Both of these statements mirror one another inversely.

What we find, in the physical sense through practicing sitting still, is the immeasurable expanse between the nature of good and evil. Once we come to believe in this concept, we also perceive that we can never pinpoint this locale. It moves out of the physical world, into the spiritual, only to reappear in a different place in its own time frame.

Wisdom is not an outcome, but a process. It's not that ultimate truth changes, but our moment-to-moment perspective is relative to that flow of energy.

In the middle of the day, without warning, every inmate is ordered to leave their place of work, education, or leisure and return to their housing unit. Once outside, I can see staff members standing in critical places on the compound to expedite the order safely.

In a matter of minutes we are all inside our units. Staff members, those we never see walking the halls, participate in a cube-by-cube count. Correctional officers follow with another count. This one is based on bed position and inmate number.

Before and after the count, there are many discussions of various thoughts and feelings. The gamut varies from inmate to inmate. As in meditation, I go to the space to listen to all of the perspectives. In this place of quietude, there is no judgment, only an inventory of diverse reactions to the count.

From an emotional perspective:

- There are those who seemed obviously angry at the sudden change in routine.
- There are others who joked and seemed unaffected by the order.
- Then, there are those who remained silent during the operation.

From a thought perspective:

- There are those who speculated about why such a count had to be conducted. The theories are numerous and the conversations are colored with expletives.
- There are others who seem transfixed on what was not being accomplished because of their absence from work, class, or leisure.

- Then, there are others who read a book, work on a puzzle, or disclose their pleasure over the sudden break in their routine.

The angry, speculative crowd seems largest, and of course, the loudest. The jokers and those transfixed by worry over what was not being accomplished is a smaller mix. Those who are silent are a very small minority. What I can ascertain from these men is purely speculative.

What I experience in the whole matter is peace. Who, why, positive, or negative of the event doesn't matter. I am not overjoyed or angry, but I can be compassionate to every single response – whether it is a drill, or there is a blunder to be fixed. The reason doesn't matter because, in less than two hours, it is over and the rest of the day proceeds as it always does.

The wisdom I found was in understanding every single projection and reaction as normal for that person's relative perspective to their genetics, learning history, and their current ability to see clearly and express compassion for those moments.

Just for today, I can let go and let God. Is this enlightenment? Perhaps it is only a glimpse.

February 16th

Being aggressed upon brings up fear, anger, and possible self-doubt. Every moment is a teacher. The wisdom is to give it space enough to make the most peaceful decision. The key is to stay centered and work the issue from the inside out. The answer is never between you and the other person. It is between you and the Universal mind. Time allows us to experiment with this balance. To respond aggressively is a basic tool of survival; however, the opportunity to address one's anger has so many possibilities. Pausing long enough to be aware of anger is a courageous choice. Right and wrong is a very narrow truth. There are higher choices of reasoning. Choosing to love one's self and one's neighbor takes practice. We can prepare for this by rehearsing these new choices in our minds, in advance. When we become angry we close down. Our options become limited. Opening up to experience anger creates compassion and kindness for ourselves. We come to understand a new view of how to relate to the world.

I fear angry people. This horror goes back pretty far. This is the past. I can break free of the chains of my own mind by concentrating and making friends with my fear. Instead of reacting to this fear with mental anguish, I just sit with the darkness of fear. I drop it in the space. I am making a decision to make some progress in my life by allowing what I feel to simply be.

I am developing relaxation and open awareness. I see clearly. I allow the energy of compassion to flow as it wishes.

This is not under my control. I slowly let go and allow God to show me how this works! I can't really love my neighbor unconditionally, until I love who I am first! I was told not to love myself, that to do so is selfishness. That's a thought I let go of. This is now! I am looking, not at the person that I believe causes my fear, but at fear itself, without an object. All I need is my breath to stay anchored.

February 17th

The space that we create during meditation can be used after our practice. If we don't achieve our path, we inventory what mistakes we made and we learn something new about ourselves.

Steadfastness comes with patience. Detachment with love allows those we have offended the time it takes to deal with their own feelings and discursive thoughts. We all have different paths. The only focus is on the course we are taking.

A few members of the group have become angry with me for supposedly "sticking my nose in where it doesn't belong" at work. A correctional officer gave me a direct order to tell these inmates to do a task. The outcome was very unpleasant. They believe I am the instigator of the command.

This splinters the social relationships I've created, so I experiment with anger and fear by reaching out to others, all the while being confused about who to trust in prison. I back away quietly, even from the people I am close to, in order to see my own patterns for making friendships.

I break an inmate code by going to a correctional officer to share with him the boundaries I need to set with the inmates who are angry with me. I have tried to solve the situation directly and nothing has been resolved. I go to the psychologist and she encourages me to continue looking at my own behavior as the only focus for cheating steadfastness.

I choose to act in the middle, after spending time alone to sit with fear, anger and my own self-doubt. I reach out to some neutral inmates to present the larger picture without blame. The answer that comes is the same. Give the predicament time, while breathing compassion and kindness in both directions – inward and outward.

After asking for help, I make the decision to detach from those people who are angry with me. However, I speak honestly with the men in my social circle (those with which I have greater intimacy). Instead of reflexively letting go of their friendships, to appease the men who were angry with me, I choose to reason out ways to eliminate judgment of either myself or the angered men. I make a decision to continue my commitment to those I trust with friendships. Now, I let go of that which I can't change and concentrate on the courage to change the thing I can – me.

February 18th

When angry, there are so many possibilities for response. If we pause long enough to accept the anger that has arisen within us, we can find the most peaceful way of delivering it for the good of the community. By creating that space, we can more clearly and honestly see the next step of action.

The address of this space of what we can call God is not some place in the sky. It is in the true heart, the highest place within.

I write the first statement on paper and place it on the wall next to the place where we line up for meals in the POD. The second phrase I leave on all six tables where we have our meals.

Immediately, someone goes around to all six tables and crumples up the messages. This is a single choice. The question I ask myself is what other options are available as decisions to carry out? The Universal mind commands me to experiment. On the highest level of understanding, what if there is no judgment?

By making a list of possible responses, I expand to see the ultimate truth. I come to know it because I experience it in my gut of intuition.

When I look at my list, and place my ego in a perspective of surrender, the course of action comes to me. If, after I have made a decision, the course does not create peace within me, I chalk it up to experience with the greater power of our understanding, and I move on to the next possible moment with greater discernment.

One of my greatest challenges in this process is admitting how I feed my emotions with compulsive thoughts. Confessing this character defect is half of the battle. Now, I continue to resolve being conscious of this behavior, then giving myself a break in space and adding compassion.

This is the process of letting go and letting God; the empowerment of the spirit through experimentation. The reaction of the inmate to my placing the phrases is none of my business. I vow to practice courage and place the phrases on the tables tomorrow.

February 19th

Our feelings come from within us. Our feelings are fed by our thoughts. Our thoughts fuel our words. Our words fuel our actions. Our actions fuel our patterns of behavior. Our behavior determines our life's work. Our life's work determines our destiny. Behold how great a matter a little fire kindles.

In the physical world there are opposites – right and wrong, good and evil. We would not understand short without tall, or day without night. In the spiritual world there are no opposites. What exists just is. There is no time. There is no space. Energy comes from this vacuum into the physical world and eventually goes back from where it once came. What do we do with this energy we call feelings? Normally, we react to them when our ego is in control.

Let's take a look at the phrase "I am." If "I" is in the physical world, with our body, our flesh; then "am" must exist in the spiritual world. We can tell we're in this body. We can see ourselves in the mirror. The ego experiences time and space. When we experience the energy of a feeling state, our first reaction is to close down and protect "I."

Normally, our ego is in the foreground and the "am" part, the spiritual part, is in the background. But the "am" in us never changes. It just is. What if we moved the spiritual part, the part of us that is constant, to the foreground and the ego to the background? We begin to observe ourselves. We begin to awaken. Our awareness expands our vision of the sacredness of The Universe. This starts with us, with "I" making a decision to surrender to consciousness.

Now is the moment for allowing the spiritual to feed me, observing when I run into the walls of emotional pain located in the physical world. I admit feelings are energy. I'm practicing allowing them to arise, like an itch without scratching.

Now is the moment to accept my thoughts, then let them go. I choose to call it "thinking" instead of giving them a positive or negative connotation. Sitting still to allow this energy to flow through me is a conversion from my mind to my heart – ceasing reaction.

I'm sparsely aware of the words I use which come from my compulsive thoughts, but I know I can't stop them perfectly today. I have to experiment, watching what I think and observing what I say. Judgment comes from my thoughts and not my heart.

My faith and hope is that my words can change and that I can see what effect they have on my actions. The key lies in the focus of my consciousness, allowing this space to change my patterns of behavior. To me, this is going to the "spiritual gym." I'm not going to grow all the muscles I need by working out the first time.

The process is slow. This gentleness is new for me, along with compassion. When I suddenly see a direction to take in my life, this is devised destiny that comes from within me. I look forward to my life flowing more smoothly, with a greater sense of fulfillment. All I need is a commitment to a willingness to practice.

February 20th

Imagine the possibility that there is only one soul. We reject the idea that, since we're in separate bodies, we can be connected. If so, when we judge one another, we're really judging ourselves. We are now all worthy of the kindness and compassion that starts with an internal action.

If every human being is connected to a collective soul, then gaining wisdom is the path to follow. Coming to understand who we are takes time and discipline. There also has to be a large dose of gentleness in the discovery. We are our own worst critic. This sense of unworthiness commonly spills over into our lives while we are trying to control pain. Unfortunately, it usually only worsens the situation.

Now is the perfect time to test and find truth within us. If society labels us as good for nothing, are we aware how avidly we soak this up as our own reality? The answer lies buried deep below our hardened hearts within layers of learned false beliefs.

Perhaps it is time to practice the imaginable phrase, "Other people's opinions of me are none of my business." When we take on someone else's judgment, we take away their responsibility for their own path to wisdom. We do this with the hope of steadfast faith. The practice of loving our neighbors as ourselves becomes necessary as we empathize with the same errors we also commit. We must keep coming back to the mirror as we face what is put on our plate at (in) the moment.

As I am entering M.'s room to ask him a question, I notice T. standing with his back to me in the doorway. Normally, I avoid this individual, but today I enter anyway, saying the phrase, "God Bless You T." I quietly step past him.

T. flies into a rage, telling me, "I told you to stop talking to me." Again, I reply, "God bless you T." He pulls out the big guns and bellows, calling me a faggot and a heretic. The conversation seems one-sided and I hear his rejection loud and clear.

"Would you also like it if I stopped coming to church," I ask? "Yes you faggot, you took my fucking seat." (The Sunday before I attended church where T., finding me sitting in the section to the right of him, left the service).

As he continues his preaching, I remain silent, giving the state of affairs as much space as I can, concentrating on my breath, respecting his desire. Other than ignoring T.'s opinion of me as none of my business, I look deep to confront the enemy that bars kindness and compassion. What I find is bitterness.

If I allow the energy of bitterness to harden my heart, love has nowhere to flow. T. has been on my meditation and prayer list for some time (weeks), breathing in the darkness while breathing out compassion and tender-loving kindness. Today, I discover this dark cloud as bitterness. This betrayal is from a member of the church I attend.

T.'s opinion of my meditation, study and practice, learning from many sources other than the Bible, is a bone of contention for him. What I need is courage to acknowledge my own bitterness and to allow it to be replaced by grace.

I ask a few members of the church for help, not to condemn T., but to deal with the emotion of bitterness so that I might achieve progress over the matter. The sentiment I receive echoes the message of peace that rises within my heart. I continue to pray, in silence for T., giving him the grace that flows through me from the space.

If T. and I are connected to one collective soul, focusing my attention on dropping the rock of bitterness over to the openness of grace sends love and balance to my neighbor and myself. The wisdom of holding onto a grudge would only harden my heart and disconnect me from the soul.

February 21st

There is a difference between someone crossing our boundaries and, when we see something that we believe needs correcting, telling them they should or shouldn't be doing something that does not directly affect us. The way we come to understand the difference is an increase in consciousness.

Setting a boundary creates humility. When our egos are too small, we feel less than, disconnected from the whole. When our egos are too big, we can't actively listen to balance, because we believe we are the whole. Herein lies missing the mark, expressing self-righteousness. From this perspective, we believe we know how others ought to be acting to bring peace to the whole.

The phrase of the imposer starts with "you should." And may I be bold? "Shoulding" on someone is like shitting on them. By pausing long enough to determine what we're feeling, then giving the emotion the space to support us toward the best course of action, we are provided with the transparent honesty between what belongs to us and what belongs to them.

On a deeper level, if we are all connected, we see clearly that the solution to any given problem is between us and the space – not between us and them. We can ask for help, act appropriately, and then practice letting go of the outcome. We comprehend the efficiency of looking in the mirror, over the long haul, and determine to work only on us.

Feel free to add to this List of Instances, where boundaries could be set and the instances where shoulding exists.

Set a Boundary	Shoulding
Someone bolts in front of you in the meal line.	You shouldn't be writing these messages.
Someone takes your personal property.	You should be drinking more water.
Someone threatens to assault you.	You should clean the tables better.
Someone yells in your ear.	You should go on a diet.
Someone "shoulds" on you.	You should do as I say (and not as I do is the underlying message of hypocrisy).

There are many men in prison willing to break the rules. But unless it affects me directly, it's truly none of my business. The wisdom I'm working on is: when do I set a boundary with someone else and when do I let go and let this ultimate force of truth and sagacity take over?

The key, for me, is to apply humility to my own actions, becoming aware of what emotion I'm working with and any possible character defect that needs removing.

N. spends many of his conversations declaring who works well with him and why. This one is lazy and won't lift a finger. That one is just slow, and this other man has been in the system so long he's damaged beyond repair. Of close associates he strongly suggests they should eat to lose weight. In short, he's a brilliant man with a lot of opinions.

When he comes at me with his superiority, I've tried patience and detachment. When his shoulding starts to affect me personally, I set a boundary, sometimes imperfectly. I lose my temper and, later in the day, have a seat to see what shortcomings I need to have removed.

I can learn from this man by taking the high road. I have practiced detaching from him, knowing full well how my weakness arises for grasping. All the while, I keep faith and hope alive by asking the wisdom mind to bestow blessings upon him, focusing on compassion and tender-loving-kindness.

Lastly, it's very important for me to take the high road, should I "perceive" him to be attempting to push my buttons. For these occasions, I need to admit my ego wants to project why he's acting in a particular way, and frankly, I can never know for sure.

If he's not respecting my boundary of keeping his distance from me, I just breathe and wait for the storm cloud to dissipate. Between setting boundaries and shoulding, detachment with love is a sure fire way to practice creating peace for everyone concerned.

February 22nd

Regardless of what brought us to this point, we have lost so much, in terms of personal connections, the ability to earn a living and familiar places. On top of that, we have to make sense of the honesty about why we are here. We have to get past societal opinions and the judgment of some correctional officers. (For those living on the outside, it would be the opinions of bosses, family and friends.) Even fellow inmates deliver their own brand of condemnation to one another. Grieving over all of this takes time and incredible fortitude. It takes guts!

We have to create balance. It is a time to let our old selves die and to take on a rebirth of self. We can be the phoenix that rises out of the ashes of its former body. We can produce a new us, one small step at a time by practicing being awake to all that we can be.

We can imagine these new details: the physical, the mental, the emotional and the spiritual. We can sit for a while and choose NOW goals for ourselves. But we also have to let go of ego. Once we see clearly what we wish to become, we can let go and take steps in any new direction to decide what fits with our new vision.

As we nourish this moment, we come to feel a sense of self-love that fills the holes where loss has left its mark. We don't achieve anything through willpower. All we have to do is open our awareness and put one foot in front of the other. The creating force within will guide us and we begin to experience the fulfillment of love.

Suddenly, it dawns on me that I practice meditation to see my being. I want to know who I really am! This sacredness fills me up and overflows to others. I am learning to give unconditionally, regardless of any response. I am becoming more alive than ever before. I am casting off the idea that I am a mistake. I make mistakes and am learning from them.

I have the power to overcome. I write to capture the process. I meditate to move forward into my destiny. It is a valuable usage of time. All I need is my faith!

February 23rd

What if we changed the focus when it comes to emotional expression and experience? When we see something we like or dislike, our mind develops a memory of such. The past has the effect of setting up a reaction that is similar to what we have already encountered. In the present moment, we start at ground zero, observing the feeling state that arises within us, focusing away from the object causing the emotion and moving towards observing the emotion itself.

Instead of following the thoughts that feed the feeling (that have been constructed by our desires), we can practice a pattern of observing the emotion as the target. Then we can make a decision to turn our willingness toward examining the intensity and texture of passions that arise within us. In doing so, we own the emotion 100%.

Going deeper, let's imagine spending time in a place where many of the objects of our desires are absent. Wait a minute! We're already doing that here in prison. Let's go further, to a place where there's solitary confinement. Now, what happens to us? We're stuck with only our minds. But our minds are conditioned to having something with which to relate. Our minds create thoughts to substitute for what's absent. The end result is loneliness and a great depth of sadness.

Developing the discipline to focus on the emotional state which emanates within us, the space we give it allows for new patterns of behavior to develop. In short, we come to know solitude because, as every moment passes, eventually it dissolves all by itself. The intensity/solidity of any emotion changes over time. We come to understand the relativity of that feeling based on the perspective we feed it.

I'm on the A side of the unit and I miss the midnight count! I react immediately with fear, guilt, and shame. I have made a mistake by not being in my cubicle on the B side according to the institutional rules. My lack of compassion and forgiveness for myself are an ingrained habit that goes all the way back to my childhood. The mistakes I make are never forgiven in my mind. Over time, these mistakes are brought to my attention over and over, as if they are stuffed in a bag that I am forced to wear on my back. Once I go back to the B side, I immediately go to the correctional officers and apologize for my mistake. Practicing in the present moment, I risk asking for forgiveness. I am going right into "I AM" meditation, all the while my thoughts are wild with self-hatred, intensifying the fear. Since I am a really well-behaved inmate, I am excused for my mistake. Tonight, I asked for help (an act of courage) not depending on the outcome. In the present moment, the correctional officer offers me grace. He isn't my father. He doesn't force me to shove this mistake in the bag on my back. Instead, I am practicing new behaviors and I get different results. I take my seat on my bed and feel amazing gratitude. I could have been sent to isolation, but that is a thought! The space allows me to practice self-forgiveness, compassion, and tender-loving-kindness. I sleep really well after my evening meditation.

February 24th

Where in the world can you find a forest without a dead tree? The answer is nowhere. Perfectionism is a spiritual disease. A decaying tree provides shelter for creatures; it nourishes the rest of the living trees, as it decays into the forest floor. We can take a lesson from this. Human error is fertilizer for increased intimacy. What we see as a problem is really a chance to develop a closer bond with those we love and those who love us. It may be our predestination for future successes. People who cannot see this have not yet learned the lesson of forgiveness. We can learn to forgive ourselves, first by taking responsibility for our actions, learning what we can, and making amends to those involved. We humbly pick up the pieces and plant them in the new garden of our souls. We do this so we can be open to receive love again.

We learn more from our mistakes than we do our successes. We can tell ourselves it's okay to make an error. Then, we can forgive our failures and store our successes. Imperfection is part of the Universal design, but we don't dwell on it, once we have memorized the lesson.

It is the 10 AM count. C/O L. is asking the inmates to stand, when we normally don't do so for this count. I do what I'm told because I'm just not interested in any drama. When Mr. R is asked to stand, his answer is "NO"! What happens next is predictable. Mr. R is hauled off to the SHU (Segregation Housing Unit- they don't call it the hole or isolation anymore). There is imperfection everywhere. Mr. R is no longer a human being. Mr.

L. is acting out of black and white thinking. Both of these men need compassion and tender-loving-kindness. This is prison. My spiritual foundation to practice is a choice to avoid the pitfalls of aggression, craving and ignorance. There is no discussion between these two men today. The wisdom I receive is to practice forgiveness for both of these men, then move on with my day. These men are responsible for their own spiritual welfares. I am not here to fix them. My "fixing" behavior is what got me into prison in the first place. Before leaving this lesson, I pause and come to know that a deeper wisdom is to forgive myself for witnessing this painful event. I take on other people's pain! Once I see this clearly, I must practice letting compassion and kindness to pass through me, then on to others.

February 25th

The energy of spite is like a suicide bomber handing out judgment to get even. It never works because it explodes on the deliverer, as well as the delivered. If we sit with the hurt and breathe out kindness and compassion, there is no fuel to spread the fire of anger. This hurt will pass, just like the tide around the phases of the moon.

When someone hurts us, it's normal to want to get even. But if we give in to spite, we fall into the enemy's trap of being the victim. What if we choose to rise above our opponent and allow the energy of the harm done to us to touch our hearts? This brings us, finally to a place of sadness that only God can heal. This is not the route of the ego, for it only seeks to protect the one.

In doing so, the tide of hurt rises and crashes, destroying everything in its path. Spite is a weapon of mass destruction. It affects all of us eventually. Regret usually follows.

If we give the pain a focused point in time and drop it there, we can ask The Universe for help. Then we can practice letting go, while giving The Universe a chance to answer us. This process takes time and patience, encouraging us to see our strides forward. This is the path of the spiritual warrior.

For several days now, N. seemed consumed with his passion for who is right and who is wrong. On several occasions, he gets his "group" together to pontificate his perspective. Since meeting this man, I spend many a day listening to his criticism of this person or that one.

This is the second time we've collided, where his inventory-taking seeps into the arena of doing my time. Experimenting with setting a firm boundary, I continue to distance myself from him.

Desperately he tries to coerce mutual friends to his side. I detach with as much care as I can. The urges to get even creep into my thoughts; however, I continue to take the high road. The more he tries to bad mouth me in front of my friends, the more I give him the freedom to spend time with them out of respect.

I begin to pray and make a mental list of all the positive things this man does in his life. I refuse to bad mouth him in front of our confidants. I encourage the acceptance of this man, while doing my best to be kind to him from a distance. I know my own peccadilloes and since I cannot change him, I practice acceptance, by looking at the hurt I feel without the focus of blaming either him or myself.

The compulsive thoughts that arise are fierce, but I continue to only be aware of them, giving my anguish as much space as I can muster in the present moment.

I encourage one fellow, frustrated over the tension between us, to join me in the high road of prayer and the honor of N., asking for patience while The Universe shares the secret of its plan in time.

There is no winner or loser in this occurrence. What I experience is an absence of spiteful action on my part, while moving from loneliness to solitude. Through courage of my spiritual practice, I do not have to lose another comrade.

February 26th

How many times have we heard the phrase "patience is a virtue?" How do we practice patience? How is the experience comprehended? Staying still and allowing thoughts and feelings to arise, without reaction, allows for first hand exposure to patience.

One of the biggest inmate codes is "Do your own time!" Deep down, this code contains more truth than might appear on the surface. It involves giving up the need to control others. We begin to believe and act as if we know what is best for our neighbor. From this construct, we begin to manipulate and control others as targets for our own happiness.

The miracle of the outcome of practicing patience is not the focus, it is our awareness of the ego's desire to dominate what thoughts and feelings arise. Giving what emanates from our minds the space to just be, we can lighten up as an exercise in experience.

For months, I supported J. compassionately as he struggled with his compulsion toward the sexual predator that exposes himself in the darkness and the night. It isn't my position to tell him what to do. He doesn't need a mother. What I need is patience.

I've learned, behind the razor wire, to continue my meditation time, clearly seeing the lesson before me – my own compulsion to fix someone else.

In the early morning hours, J. comes bounding into the cube to announce the delight of his success. In the midst of the predator following him to the bathroom to "show him his junk," J. made a decision to walk to the other bathroom.

What I gain is the fruits of letting go and letting God. This is progress for J. and a victory for patience on my part. I have witnessed a miracle for both of us.

February 27th

Treat others as we wish to be treated. Compassion is putting on someone else's shoes and seeing life through their eyes before we make a decision to act. Focusing on the hurt takes us to the core of our inner being. Now that we see and feel the pain, we can choose to remove the labels and unlock the door to a larger view of reality.

What is the worst thing about being in prison? We see so many things that are wrong in here. We spend countless moments going over how we want things improved. Now, we look at ourselves. Don't we secretly wish others would overlook our faults, forgive us, and have compassion for us as human beings? Maybe the worst thing about being in prison is the narrow focus we have when we hurt. Let's add compassion and see what happens.

Forgiveness starts with ourselves and then flows to others. As a stream feeds a river, that in turn feeds our bays, soon our compassion for forgiveness swells to the seas and oceans that ebb and flow with a greater peace.

Our attitude about being in prison can change, but we have to believe in the larger picture. That takes faith. Start by trusting in the wisdom inside us.

As inmates, we tend to hang around only "our kind." When I listen as compassionately as I can, there's always criticism launched at other groups or particular persons. Instead of launching my disapproval at the finger pointers, I make a decision not to use any outward judgment. It's an opportunity to inventory my tendency to perpetrate the same negative attribute.

- When do I say, "someone is full of shit"?
- How often do I consider someone lazy?
- When do I pull the race card?
- How often do I put someone down to build myself up?
- When do I push my own opinion in my need to be right?
- When do I further gossip?
- Do I defame someone else's character?
- Who do I consider to be less than?
- Who do I consider to have worse behaviors than mine?
- Where is my focus when I hear criticism – on them or compassionate?
- Whose crimes are worse than mine?
- Who or what do I blame for my unhappiness?

I begin to look at the truth in the belief that in order to be forgiven for all my wrongs, I must develop the action of having the compassion to forgive. The reality is, my actions hurt other people too, sometimes unintentionally. I am really no different than anyone else. Centering myself with a single breath seems to be the key. It starts with a single pause. As I sit here on my bed, looking inward for the solution for compassionate treatment, I understand it starts with a single drop of moisture that heals and nourishes my own heart.

From the inside, I can see all the clouds of negativity and judgment hiding the sun of forgiveness and the sky of compassion. The winter of my discontent with others, turned inward, becomes the Spring of the rebirth of a kind, loving human being.

I'm only hurting myself when I criticize those around me. It is a natural tendency, because of my narrow focus. Being aware of this tendency is the beginning of change. Forgiveness showers down upon my heart, so that it may flow to others and create unity.

February 28th

What annoys us? Can we just take a moment to look at pain with a wider view? Our spiritual muscles are sore from the exercise. Being aware and owning this emotion completes the training. Feed the soul and the ache heals faster. We come to believe that all answers arrive from within us.

When we go to the gym, we wait a day or two to let our sore muscles heal and rebuild, before we begin again on that specific part of our body. An annoyance works our spiritual muscles. If we continue to feed our aggravation with our thoughts and opinions, the soreness grows.

What if we pause long enough to let the emotion sit within us and let our spirit heal the ache? This is a different kind of exercise program, one that strengthens and increases our stamina for tolerance of other people's flaws. The space we create shows us we all have something that ticks off somebody else.

Happiness does not have to depend on others. We can choose to pass over a small flaw that will disappear from our memories in ten minutes. When we develop tolerance for others, we become gentler as we look inside ourselves.

I'm still new at practicing compassion and patience and creating that space reflexively in the moment. When someone gets in my face with a comment that pushes my buttons, I'm aware that my body constricts and my heart starts to pound. However, my knee-jerk retort is not always unconditionally filled with tender-loving-kindness.

Boundary setting, for me, helps me to tolerate another man's flawed insults, while assisting in creating equity in an unbalanced relationship. Overcoming self-doubt is number one on my list of character flaws and becoming more conscious of this defect is progress in itself.

After the confrontation, communicating forgiveness is important to me, even if the opposition has a closed heart and ears. Walking the track, replacing the past incident with the present moment, I celebrate the awareness of exercising my body, while dropping every compulsive thought that enters my mind.

I choose to recite a list of what I have for which I am grateful. I can't change that I'm drawn to control negativity, but at least I'm aware of my body's reaction, my compulsive thoughts, and how they feed my feelings of self-doubt.

Taking a breath and starting over with this gratitude list, I blurt out the following statement, "I'm grateful for my willingness to change." A small surge of compassion fills my heart and I sense an instance of healing. I pass that gift to my oppressor. I continue to practice letting go and letting God.

February 29th (Leap Year)

During meditation practice, we are becoming more comfortable with watching ourselves. We see our ego. We don't judge it. We just observe and go back to the breath of the present moment of who we are.

Then, just for a moment, we can explore watching the watcher! There, all movement ceases and peace emanates from within us. This is a still, calm, wise place. We don't think our way to this place. We just are, when we shift to this vast emptiness.

Everything is invited here. This is the consciousness of pure acceptance and serenity. We cannot capture it. It escapes any measure of control. Instead, we come to know surrender.

Watching: I AM.

March 1st

Sh.t/g.d d.m./m. th f..k.h b.tc. Words themselves are not good or bad. Perhaps the question is: what emotion do these words help us feed? If we remove the words as speech or thought and sit quietly with the feeling, we become more awake. We begin to solve the energy from within. As a wise inmate said, "It's your mouth!"

We have learned to react to the words we have grown up hearing. These phrases become part of the recipe for the same meal our ego will digest over and over. It never complains, because it is our familiar coping mechanisms.

With meditation, we can start fresh. Every moment can become an unlimited banquet, as we watch ourselves create new recipes with old leftovers. We can suddenly see new words to express the space between passion and aggression, fame and disgrace, praise and blame, and pain and pleasure.

Using old worn out words to express negative emotions does not make us any happier. There is so much more to chew on that is healthier and inventive. What will we eat today?

Being less prone to use the repeated phrases that I hear over and over, my main undertaking is to be more compassionate for those stuck in the revolving door of profanity usage. It's much easier to judge and blame people for their ignorance, than to look beneath the surface to address the painful experience we all share.

It seems clear to me that someone addicted to profanity is just as worthy of compassion. The solution seems to be in creating space between the two factions, with both parties focusing on the more peaceful horizon of balance.

Neither the users of profanity, nor the co-addict, attempts to change the person in front of them. Acceptance and a mirror are the tools for greater tender-loving-kindness. For both parties, there is but one truth: “It’s my mouth!”

March 2nd

We can face our problems with fear and anger, or with loving-kindness and compassion. An opinion of any given situation is not owned by anyone, other than the one who delivers it. Rather than jumping to a fast conclusion, based on what we think, we can become still. Then, a peaceful resolve will come.

There's nothing wrong with feeling anything. Bad circumstances can be changed into a situation that adds to the increased intimacy between two people. It is an opportunity to become more aware of who we are.

Spending time with our feelings, practicing total ownership, and then communicating from a place of compassion, we begin to open up to the truth about reality.

Our egos have opinions. They constrict us. If the focus is on our spirit, there are no losers because we are all one in the spirit. Growing kindness swallows everything painful and allows it to bear its fruit.

Practicing the actions of kindness and compassion brings us a new wisdom, but we can't just think it. We learn by doing. We act through faith, keeping an eye on those who have come before us.

Saying "no" for my own self-esteem is the hardest action for me to practice in prison. Pleasing people put me in here. Self-doubt destroys my life.

Someone asks me to pick up a certificate. He earned it for a group in which I also participate. Pushing my focus away from his wish to avoid personal responsibility, my heart still leads me to say no, because I do not wish to enable him.

Working through my own fear of the outcome is my intention, not the desire to punish him. Giving in would mean acting out within the same issue that put me in prison. I reflexively wish to fix other people's desires, so they'll think more highly of me. When I say no to being an enabler, people get angry. Some get even with a spiteful vengeance.

This is my decision to make. I base it on the quiet stillness of looking at self-doubt and fear of disapproval directly and allowing that energy to swell up inside me (on an imaginary wall I've built within my heart).

Later in the evening, I ask him if we can talk about his anger, and he tells me that his trust level between us has dropped, mostly because I would not do what he asked of me, nor did I give him a reason as to why. I accept that fact. At first, he is not interested in my side; however, as I listen, he opens up. I share my fear of his being angry with me if I say no and I let it go at that.

Then, something awesome occurs. He says he forgives me, when I ask for a pardon. “It is what it is, and it’s in the past. I don’t hold grudges.” In listening and sharing, I keep a friend, without having to people please. I experience a greater sense of intimacy.

March 3rd

One day, in the middle of the night, two dead inmates got up to fight. Back to back they faced each other, drew their swords and shot each other. The deaf C/O heard the noise and came and shot the two dead inmates. If you don't believe this story is true, ask the blind snitch. He saw it too! Spirituality has to have humor.

The prison experience is filled with negativity; however, constant focus on the prophecy of doom leads to a life out of balance. We can learn to diffuse situations, lessening anxiety and tension, by observing who, what, where, and why. We can begin looking at the larger perspective to disarm a life of pessimistic focus.

Entertainment can have an unexpected twist, not just for us, but for others as well. There are those with whom we can be humorous and others not. One inmate described humor as "you doing time," not "time doing you."

Another inmate spoke in humor to say, "I live in a gated community where the rent is great. If I can deal with difficult people in here, when I get out, dealing with outside people will be a piece of cake."

Does humor manifest from a natural life of joy, or does it arise to mask and subdue the pain of prison? Can it be both?

Two humorous events happened today that brought me a sense of enjoyment. In one instance, I was able to laugh at myself.

Sitting on my bed, focused on an exercise of meditation, I heard an inmate singing "Jingle Bells." It's March and Spring is around the corner. Hearing the music brought me a sense of joy that I shared with the expanded world around me.

I saw a soap dish in the front shower yesterday and I really wanted it. It appeared to have a full bar of soap. I said to myself, "Don't steal!" I saw it again this morning. I reminded myself not to take what's not mine, even though the urge to grab it arose again as a thought.

After spending time on the rec yard, I came inside to take a shower before the 4 PM count. I went into my locker to get my shower bag. My soap dish was missing from the tote. I went back to the shower area…it was my soap dish!

March 4th

Someone once said, "We have two ears and one mouth. Perhaps it is because we can practice listening twice as much as we speak." If we cannot listen to someone now, we should ask ourselves when? Opening up to someone else's pain doesn't mean we own it. It still belongs to them. By listening, a deeper connection becomes the solution.

We all exhibit positive and negative attributes. By listening, there is an opportunity to see how we will react to what another person says or does. Silence, while listening, keeps the focus on our side of the street. We can achieve a more peaceful balance for everyone concerned.

There is a brilliant man in our unit. I avoid him because he chronically tells others, me included, "you need to do this," "you should or shouldn't do this," projecting outcomes that are none of his business.

Instead of judging him from a distance, I do several things while listening to him pontificate:

- I do my own time and I give him space to do his time in the way he sees fit. I detach with love.
- I make a point to be compassionate by making a mental note of the many positive attributes he displays, so I can see him as a whole person. This creates balance.
- I look at my own life and assess my own inventory, using his iniquity as a golden opportunity to see if I am exhibiting the same conduct. If I find myself having a

> feeling of resentment, I own that feeling 100% and allow it to dissolve in the space of silence.

Earlier in my bid (this is a term for a prison sentence) a certain man starts to tell me what I should do to achieve balance. I told him “no.” I set a firm boundary. When he continued, I blurted out the truth that I didn’t need a mother. This angered him terribly. He told me so later – and let me know I am not to call him “mother”. I listened, and to this day, I have not repeated the offense.

I’m on the road to wisdom when I accept someone who pushes my buttons of resentment and judgment. By avoiding him, I can “do my time with the right mind.” People who pass judgment and try to control another’s behavior need my compassion. I’ve been there and done that. I just breathe in the darkness and breathe out the joy and balance of being. By listening to others, I’m actually listening to myself and celebrating our connection to the whole.

March 5th

When you look at someone, do you see their faults or do you see who they are? Our egos seek to make oneness with what other people do. Our spirit only seeks to see, through all our doing, who people are. Once we see who we are, we become connected to the whole.

It's not hard to find fault with other inmates or staff as we focus on the things that get on our very last nerve. But if we concentrate only on those flaws, we will never get to see the good that we do. The wisdom is balance. All of us have good and bad actions that we play out each and every day.

Here is a spiritual truth and a note of caution. If we see only the wrong in others, guess what? We secretly see only the bad in ourselves. Let's all meet in the center of calm and peace. This is the real joy of living.

I avoid people who constantly take inventory of other people's faults. It's not to punish them, but to detach with love. I would rather pray for and extol those people from a distance, allowing them the freedom to be who they are today.

Concentrating on the mirror, rather than getting involved in changing others, I am making sure I'm not criticizing them or myself too harshly. With detachment, the space not only gives me the ability to observe myself more objectively, but the insight I receive through the experience helps me skillfully practice the wisdom that is given to me. Acting wisdom into a new way of being shifts the gravity of who I am.

By continuing to take personal inventory of my assets and defects of character, I can see past my opinions and discern that who I am connects to the entirety. Living, based on my emotions, relies on something that is foolish – impermanence.

P. is someone I avoid. He criticizes my spiritual practice to others behind my back. This is only part of who he is, just as I have my faults. He sat down to dinner at the table where I was sitting, even though I specifically asked him to respect my boundaries and keep away.

The focus, now, was not whether he fulfilled his responsibility to me, but how I could overcome any character defects on my side of the street. I quietly respected his presence, talked to others, and gently took in a breath of any negativity that existed between us. I breathed out compassion and kindness for both of us.

My goal was to stay away from my mind's egotistical desire to determine why he sat diagonally from me. In reality, it was an opportunity to practice forgiveness, away from the fear of my mental perception of his vindictiveness. He is a brilliant man. I commend his abilities, as I do my own. Despite our differences, we are still connected.

March 6th

An unobserved emotion is like cooking a meal and then leaving the house with everything on the stove and in the oven. One day, the feast catches fire and burns down the house. A great dinner is tended to with great care and seasoning. Discernment helps us choose the best course of action for the whole. The emotion is served with wisdom.

It is 11:30 pm and time for lockdown count. The handbook says that all inmates are to stand by their bunks for the tally. We are instructed to get in our bunks this night. Mr. P. isn't happy. He sits on his storage box, near his bed. Again, the order is given to get in our bunks. Mr. P. does not budge. The C/O doesn't either. Words are exchanged. Someone is right and someone is wrong. Mr. P. goes to the SHU that night and doesn't come back.

The C/O reacts from a place of self-righteous anger. The inmate reacts from a place of victimhood. Neither initially observes how they feel. The issue is the energy of anger, not the absolute location of the count.

We, as inmates, do not have the power to control the rules. But we do have the power to examine our anger as if it were a meal meant to be prepared slowly. How do we see the dish being served? Yes, the C/O could have been a whole lot more flexible in the count. The lesson is that each of us is responsible for giving our emotions some space before we jump into thin air. Now we don't get to see Mr. P. laughing and filled with joy, as he plays chess with his comedic rival. Enthusiasm went to the SHU with him.

March 7th

When we blame our troubles on someone else or ourselves, everyone loses. There is another option, but it is not for the weak. Drop the blame and invite the pain in for a visit. Sit and look at it and learn the wisdom from it. Put the knowledge in our pocket and drop the pain in the vast empty space we call God. She will take it away when she sees fit. This is emotional success.

An inmate, annoyed with me cutting my toenails on a seat in the day area, turns me in to the guard for what he considers "disgusting." I have seen others cutting their fingernails on the tables and thought nothing of it. The C/O comes and confronts me, asking me to sanitize the seat. The incident leaves me with an issue to solve.

Do I blame the inmate for snitching? Do I blame the C/O for not telling the inmate to come to me as an adult to discuss his annoyance? Do I blame myself for the error of cutting my toenails on a plastic stool? I remove the nails and wipe the seat, but I am ordered to sanitize it with a solution.

I go to the inmate and apologize for my error, but that fails. He continues to be pissed off and rejects my apology.

I sit quietly with the pain, being honest with myself. I remove the blame and sit. Then, it comes to me. If I identify with the error and make it who I am, it hurts. This is a reaction, something I reflexively do. The higher wisdom is to understand that who I am is still the same. What I do is not who I am. If I forgive the situation, the pain dissolves and I go back to the rest of my evening. And I do.

March 8th

Happiness does not have to depend on others or events. Happiness is grown by opening our view and dropping opinions of what we think, regarding things that have happened. When all else fails, humor is a supply of water that douses the fire of dissatisfaction.

The laundry arrives later than normal. Inmates are questioning and complaining all day, "Where's the laundry?" Finally, at 10 pm our clothes arrive. Like a pack of wolves surrounding a fresh kill, I watch them all descend to claim their belongings.

Then, the comments come. "This f.ck.n' shit's still wet." They have all f.ck.n' day to get this done and they bring it back all f.ck.d up. This sh.t's crazy."

Happiness seems to come only from perfectly dried laundry, delivered on time, without a flaw. Everyone's laundry is in a meshed bag, so nothing is lost. It sometimes doesn't dry all the way, because it is all bunched up in the bag. The key, for me, is to watch my thinking process and let it go.

I remove my opinion and sit with the dampness. I expand my thoughts and awareness. Once I relax and my mind is steadier, the current events become more striking. Someone did laundry for me. I didn't have to do it. Someone took it away and brought it back clean. What difference does it make how late it comes back? I am not going anywhere anytime soon. After twenty minutes of lying on the bed, the laundry dries. I fold mine up and put it away.

Happiness does not come from dry laundry; it comes from opening my view and dropping my opinion. Tomorrow there will be a complaint about something else that will be forgotten in twenty-four hours. Did anyone appreciate how fresh the laundry smelled? That is the humor. The laundry is clean, but our hearts are dirty. Only I can give my soul a bath by letting go. When was the last time I cleaned up my attitude toward life? The answer, for me, is NOW!

March 9th

The wise, wonderful heroes inside each of us are waiting to come out now. Don't wait for it to surface after we leave here. The Universal Divine Mother cares not what we've done. She cares for and loves who we are. We must open our hearts to the compassion that rightly belongs to us.

Once a week we receive outside rec (short for recreation). I bring a book to read, as I am still recovering from bronchitis. We get an hour (or so) once a week to go outside in the yard, which is half the size of a basketball court. A basketball game starts. Razor wire surrounds the building on the top walls. The weather is brisk outside and the wind is playful.

But as we roll out, I can hear someone say, "Is this all there is to the outside? There's not much room here." I forget all about the book and just lie down on the concrete near the fence, watching the clear blue, cloudless sky. *"Room?"*, I say to myself. *"Why, there is* no *ceiling here."* And the sun shines so bright I can barely keep my eyes open. I spread my arms wide and just stare upwards. Then, it happens. Observing myself, I leave my body. I drift up as a kite on the wings of the chilled March breeze. I can see myself smelling both the freshness of the air and the delicate fragrance that pours from the jail's dryer vent. I watch the sun beat down on my face and arms, stroking me gently as if to say, "I love you."

The sickness I feel in my lungs seems to leave me. There is laughter in the air. The sound of a basketball echoes off the walls and joins me above the roof, past the confinement of the sharp razor spirals that surround the enclosure.

This truly is being born again; it is the second coming in each present moment that follows. There is no fear here, no anger, only peace. I could have complained that the gusts of air were too cold, but the fingers of the sun remind me again of its compassionate warmth.

Who I am is the hero. I'm the one who watches me live day-by-day. This is my true self; by just being, I am free to float away. I cannot contain my joy. Everything falls away around me. Only my heartbeat and breath remain. I am free to rise as high as I can imagine.

I rise up to join the crowd entering into the building after rec ends and the sound of sliding door to the pod closes my ears. Once inside, I sit down at the table to continue my serenity. The sun, the sky, and the wind all join me, as one, inside. It does not let go for hours. All I have to do is be still. I can accomplish anything here.

March 10th

When we resent something or someone, we try to solve the feeling with our egos - typically over and over. An emotion cannot be solved. It is energy. When we repent, we rethink the situation, so we can place it in the space of true perspective. Then, we let it go where The Universe dissolves it. All we have to do is be aware and ask for help.

An inmate falls on the bathroom floor. Stretched out, it doesn't take long for someone else to notice. Then, the reaction starts. A correctional officer moves toward the scene. His sergeant remains in his chair at the observation station. Resentment explodes over the lack of responsiveness of the superior officer and the accusations flare. Soon it becomes a battle over who is right and who is wrong, concerning this man's care. The dayroom near the accident is cleared because of the mounting tension and insinuations.

I have to take a step back and sit quietly in my own bunk, drawing in this person's pain, while exhaling a sense of peace, compassion and kindness. There is a war going on over his care. I practice harnessing all of this resentment (the slow-acting sergeant and the bellowing inmates) and molding it into a fashion that tends to all of the pain in the room. There are three human tragedies going on simultaneously: the gentleman in pain on the floor, the boisterous sergeant's defensive stance and the critical banter of inmate outrage.

Mr. H. seems to be the still focus inside the cyclone. Perhaps I am out there too, extending whatever energy I can to balance the situation. Is there anyone else in the room concentrating on the simple concept of The Universe's supreme concern? I cannot judge such. It is not my place. I look straight into the event and see the mangled cries for aid coming from all directions.

Finally, I can see it as clear as day. It is through the actions of Mr. H. He isn't verbally pushing the inmates or interfering with the ridicule of lawsuit versus dismissive hand gestures and deflective commands. He is silent, calling for help over his walkie-talkie. This is the true response – to be aware, act, and then let go.

Ultimately, the Supreme Being is in charge of both the path and the destination. I have an opportunity to look into what is, but not think of my opinion as a solution.

Too many cooks spoil the soup.

March 11th

The mind has the capability to use a fear of past experiences to destroy the consciousness of the present moment. When this happens, we can choose to look at our present fear as false evidence appearing real. This is a prime moment to separate who we are from what we think. Wisdom has no form. It expands and surrounds thoughts with a cool calmness that creates peace without force.

The new federal facility, to which I am shipped, does not have a bottom bunk that will provide for my neuro-muscular issue, so I spend my first night in the Special Housing Unit (SHU). I haven't been happy for quite some time, spending five-and-a-half months in the "hole" at the local jail. They had no other place to put me and keep me safe. That is a thought. I let that go. Being alone with a bunk all to myself is an experience in solitude; however, I have grown spiritually and I am not interested in repeating this encounter of solitary confinement. Again, this is just another thought. It is false evidence appearing real.

I accept this directive with past mental baggage in tow. Tonight is a night to practice self-kindness, then get out of my ego and hand the evening over to my broadening spirit.

This place is different. There is a greater stillness in the echo that bounces off of the cement walls. The nightly percussion of rap, found in the local jail, is not here at all. I take advantage of the shower in the room to further relax my wits, while reviewing my awareness of rambling thoughts. Be curious. Live one moment at a time.

Before long, my bed is made and the smell of fresh new cotton blankets and sheets lulls me to sleep until breakfast.

Within a few hours after lunch, my meditation finishes. I am moved to the general compound and a bottom bunk. I have my fears, although unfounded, while being face-to-face with gentleness. My ego is thankful it has listened to wisdom.

Reminding myself to brave the voice of the past, along with a vow to view the present moment from a fresh approach is a new common-sense insight: Am I appreciating myself, regardless of where I rest?

March 12th

Wisdom is very much like the phases of the moon or the chirping of a bird. These sights and sounds are always there, but we have to have our eyes and ears open to receive them. Do we know where the moon is in the sky? How the birds sing? The key is to widen our focus beyond what we do and concentrate on who we are. Are we awake? The Universe is calling us. Be still and know that I am God… Allah… Dios… Yahweh.

When a storm comes (prison), I can take some time to look at the bad weather. If I believe I am a plastic bag, the storm throws me everywhere it wishes. But if I am the sky, I only have to wait for the storm to pass. I simply ask myself, "Am I a plastic bag or the sky?" It depends on my view.

Today, I am the sky. The storm will pass. Blue sky and the sun will color my life with serenity. I no longer believe I am a plastic bag. That is self-hatred in the worst view of victimhood. Real perspective takes quiet reflection. I'm grateful to find it when I sit.

Sitting with a painful emotion, observing without reacting, takes pulling out the space of meditation to real world situations. Pausing gives me the perspective of the sky, while reacting makes me the plastic bag.

March 13h

Living in the present moment, rather than focusing on what has happened in the past, or what we cannot know will happen in the future, allows us to deal with allowing our lives to be controlled by the wisdom of our spirits or the emotions and thoughts of our egos. Sitting alone in solitude allows the definitive answer to surface, as we give ourselves the chance to ask the right questions. Allowing time to address our ego's concern, with a focus on the spirit in the "now" helps us to make the best decisions.

The man who played a sadistic, practical joke on me landed me in prison. Except God, no one really understands the whole debacle. I plead guilty on the advice of my public defender (also known inside as a public pretender). That's a thought I need to let go. I have processed this and come out whole. This man accompanies me to our final destination (on the bus) and I find it appropriate to share with him that I am not angry. God has a greater plan. I am practicing humility. It is important for me to make amends to him while I am on this trip.

G., I say, "I need to tell you that nothing I ever told you, about anything personal in the last fifteen years, was the truth. It was all made up." "SHHHH," he replies. "Someone may hear you. Pipe down! Let's not talk about this right now." That was all I needed to do for myself. I have made my amends and found peace.

Who knows how the order was written to put me in segregation? I struggle with the feelings of hopelessness. I have come to understand that time alone gives me the solitude I probably need to work on myself without any interference. But what about the pain I am feeling? I'm so past the situation with G. I feel great compassion for him, because it's important for my own spiritual development.

My ego pipes up in my mind. *"Hey, I can't leave this cell because* someone *says I have to be separated. Why do I have to be secluded?"* Now, I sit with the pain and give it to the space and wait. For nineteen days I work with my broken heart. I have not even one single urge to react. I just keep practicing what I've been reading for eight months. Here is what my spirit tells me from the space:

- When you feel like it is necessary, go back, reread this post again. Start fresh.

- You have total quiet in which to write.
- You are totally safe from harm. No one can touch you.
- All of your meals are brought to you. There is enough food!
- You have time to study and practice what you read in solitude.
- Someone was kind enough to bring you pencils.
- You have books, sent to you by people who love you unconditionally. These books will help you grow.
- You have a shower in your room.
- You have windows. You can see the grass, sky, birds and flowers.
- You have a comfortable place to sleep and meditate.
- You have the opportunity to access the space where unconditional love is unlimited. Every moment is a moment to be with yourself and take in that love.
- Wherever you are in the physical world, there will be imperfections. Your ego will not like this. That's why it's important to practice putting the ego behind the spirit, so that what is real can show itself.
- All of this shall pass. It's not permanent. Fighting against it only hurts you – no one else.
- You have what you need today. Open yourself to the compassion, kindness, and love that exists in just being.

Above all, don't take this action by another personally.

Regardless of what happens to me in this physical world, as a human being, I deserve love. I may not always receive unconditional love from others, but it is plentiful in the cornucopia of God's tender spirit.

March 14th

Willingness is an admirable trait. It is the energy that fuels our hopes, our dreams, and our goals. Willfulness can oftentimes be the force that stalls everything. We lose control of that happy-go-lucky feeling we once had, and we lose interest in everything. Even more, we lose our faith.

It takes tremendous courage to practice willingness in the middle of the sea of despair. At this moment we must be clear-seeing and gentle with ourselves. Giving up and hiding in our old habits may seem comforting, but that is not lucidity or compassion in action. In the Universal view, it is self-hatred at its best. Letting go of perfectionism allows us to make some progress with faith in mind. The rest will take care of itself.

I have purposely left this page blank for nineteen days. Now, I write two paragraphs at a time and stop. That is as much progress as I can muster. I have finished my regular day's posting and I face the lack of willingness for another project. I start yoga poses. I decide to sit for a moment and meditate on my willingness. I ask the wisdom mind for help. I have two goals to accomplish and not a drop of clarity about either.

I sit and give myself the space to finish the previous day's writing and the yoga poses: to receive the expanse of compassion. I don't know how much time elapses, as I do not have a watch.

Letting go of the chatter in my mind, I arise to take life one very small moment at a time. I don't concentrate on either of my ambitions, just move on the next right action. I open the book of yoga poses to the chapter I have been working on, while in my cell. I did not do them before dinner and my ego is going to take a pass today. *"Just make an effort,"* I tell myself. Breathing slowly, I accomplish the repetitions of the first three poses I have been practicing daily. That is progress. I have folded up a blanket and placed it on the floor. I now put it back on the bed. I take a nice shower.

After washing myself slowly, along with my one t-shirt and extra boxer shorts, I dry off. I hang my laundry to air dry, then sit down to look at this page to see what further progress I can make on my second goal. The fresh scent of soap on my skin and the feel of clean hair in my fingers gives me an uplifting nudge to bring my pencil back to task.

Almost three weeks ago, I had been in regular population for four days. I heard my name called to report to a place I did not know, so I politely asked a few of the staff where it was. I found myself outside a door asking what to do next (through a communication device outside the door).

A "white shirt" came, handcuffed me, and took me to Administrative Segregation. I had previously spent my first night there, as they couldn't find me a low bunk to accommodate my neuro-muscular issues. Nothing was discussed. I was placed, once again, in a solitary cell.

I'm in the present moment. Surprisingly, I am not angry. Will that help? I honestly don't feel angry; I feel hurt. (I don't write anything on that night. I just sleep.)

When I arise the next day, I work on a new post, meditating as I have been doing for months, and I pick up where I left off. March 14th remains unfinished. I just do not have the energy to complete it. It remains that way for the nineteen days. I need to process the event, before I can finish it.

I still do not know the specifics as to why I am here. My counselor brings me a separation agreement to sign. I asked her what it is and why I should sign it. She is evasive and insists. I ask her how long I will be here. She says, “I don’t know. You’ll have to talk to SIS (Special Investigative Services).” I accept what is and sign the paper.

The next day I fill out a request form to talk to SIS about the specifics of this scenario. After filling it out, I practice being mindful of my courage to ask for help in clarification and then I let go of the outcome.

I still hear nothing. I decide to process this issue spiritually, with the space. I ask for willingness to expand past my own ego’s hurt, because I’m locked up in Administrative Segregation alone. I begin to continue my regular practices of reading, studying, and yoga for the days that ensue. This is now. This is where I am. Acceptance is the answer to all my prayers. Everything is impermanent.

March 15th

If we see a person for what they say, what they do, or what they look like, we miss who they are. Who we are is only covered up by the physical if we are not awake. All of us are connected by who we are. We must know who we are to turn on the light.

Connecting to who we are as a primary target means moving our personalities to the background, while deriving our self-esteem from this vast, empty, magnanimous space of spiritual fulfillment that takes a behavior of stillness to emancipate.

I meet with the case manager two days after I start this entry. After our encounter, I come back to my cell to process the challenge. I have to be very careful not to react to what she did or what she said. I expressed that I thought we might be having a communication problem. Her response was, "No we're not." She seemed angry, or at least annoyed, during our first meeting. It was as if I have become aware that she is playing the role of my parent, but I feel no need to respond to her as a child.

I asked for twenty seconds to sit with myself and my adult request is granted. In quietude, I asked for my ego to be removed and for my spirit to take the foreground. I realized it was just too early for either one of us to draw any type of conclusion. We just met. I stuck to the moment, accepting her discontent. I am escorted back to my cell, papers are signed at the door, and I lay down to process the event.

Then, it hits me. Rise above the situation, whatever either of us feels, does, or says. It is a moment to rise above the emotional discontent and accept what is. I cannot change this woman's desire to control the situation. If I react as a child, I am going to lose.

Accepting what is, by signing the separation documents, becomes a decision made by the adult in me. After all, I can only change me and clean my side of the street. I can accept a moment, just as it is, without all my past baggage. Even further, I can accept the potency of now by drawing in a breath – practicing letting go of the situation.

Each moment I draw another breath is a new moment. This point in time is temporary. Then, I make the decision to move to the next instant without holding onto the previous discontent. By letting go, I can see the joy in the next meal or the color of the sky outside my window. I am already connected. I only fool myself if I allow any adverse event to narrow my focus of being human. I rise above through forgiveness, clearing the canvas to paint the next moment.

March 16th

(Silent Meditation Improves Loving Enlightenment = SMILE) All answers to life are found within ourselves. Any pain can be overcome by consciously moving the "am" part of "I Am" to the foreground, then allowing that part to expand until it surrounds the part that hurts. Bathing it with tender-loving-kindness and compassion allows for the condition of being human. This is the key to our becoming fully functional, spiritual adults.

When we detach from our egos and sit quietly with our true spirits, our view of life becomes wider and higher. We still have the same feelings as before, but our support system grows larger.

Imagine being a Central American adult who is experiencing his first snowfall. He has never been in a snow related auto accident, seen a power outage due to snow laden trees, or felt the icy pain of a snowball hitting his face.

All he sees is the wonder of it all – that is the view of the spirit. Eventually, the snow becomes dirty and the magic becomes lost in the physical world.

Sitting alone in quiet meditation allows us to feed our spirit's focus of the world. This takes work, but we can find a lot more time to give such a project when we just slow down. The question is: "Is it worth it?" We'll never know until we try. What do we have to lose?

There are so many things going on in our lives, other than what is wrong. Negativity is the spotlight of the ego. Our sights get lower and narrower until we usually explode, because the pain is all we can see. Life needs contrast, just as day needs night and happy needs sad. Enlightenment is reaching the middle road where we find peace.

Now, here's the catch. We have to learn to become our own best friend. The spiritual part of us knows how. Notice I

did not say the religious part. Religion is something we practice – we do. Our spirits are waiting to be uncovered. We only need to sit, awakening, merely being ourselves.

If we're having trouble "being," we ask someone to help who knows how to accomplish this task. They're the ones with the kindness, compassion, peace, and balance in many of the things they do. Just don't forget the human part. That makes us imperfect. As we forgive ourselves, we begin to experience forgiveness for everyone; because, after all, we are spiritually connected to the whole Universe.

In segregation, I have entire days to be my own best friend. Except for meal delivery, I am alone to practice meditation all day. I clean the room, including my own personal shower. I wash the floor. I practice yoga from the book I have. (Thank you to the Human Kindness Foundation for the chapter on Hatha Yoga). I take a shower. I eat my meal slowly. I do my best to live in the present moment all day. When I find myself creeping into the past, or wanting to know what could happen in the future, I gently remind myself to look at the list I made on March 13th. That stabilizes my mind. It is the best way to train myself in living in the present moment.

March 17th

Just be. Everyone keeps talking about living in the present moment. Well, what does that mean? Those writing and talking about this conviction share of learning from the past and, when done, the importance of letting those former moments pass. Being totally present means being emotionally, thoughtfully, physically, spiritually, and volitionally sentient.

We cannot be fully present if we hold onto the past. We miss all the present wonder, the ability to sit with what is happening right now. At the end of each day, we can mentally wash the chalk inscriptions from the board of life and start again. Sometimes, during a particularly hectic day, that means taking in a new breath and starting over at the exhale. Our souls only know now, they don't experience time.

If we are trying, in our minds, to relive the past to correct a mistake, or if we are worried about the future, we miss the serendipity of the day. We overlook the chance to feel the warmth of the sun, to appreciate the simple joy of drinking a cold cup of water, or to experience the gratitude after having a full meal. We might never get what we want today, but we can certainly widen our perspective to see what we have to be thankful for.

Jesus Christ was recorded as saying the following, "I and the Father are one." For many years, I read this in the same way - until now. Today, I see that Christ was able to do something that could not be duplicated by anyone else.

With plenty of time to devote to my own development, I receive many books on spiritual growth – from codependency all the way to the techniques of several methods of meditation. Here, I can look at all sorts of spiritual concepts, turning every book inside out on my visit to the meditation cushion. And yes, I do have a copy of the Bible.

I look at Christ's statement and take it into meditation. I am surprised as to what I find true today. If each present moment of now is the only important moment, and if I make the decision to put the spirit of a higher power in front and the ego of my desires in the background, then I, too, can see the sagacity of Jesus' words.

My spirit is connected to the Universe of God, as it is intended, observing the natural rhythm of existence. Now, I may not be able to operate 24/7 on this new revelation (I and the present moment are one), but all I have to deal with is the moment of now and face where I am. If I start compulsively ruminating, I just say "thinking," and go back to my breath.

This spiritual path has so many more options to choose from. All I have to do is be open enough to receive them. Then, I can make a decision that leads to peace of mind – for me and the world at large. The urge to be right falls away as a cause of frustration.

Just like Christians say, I can be reborn, just by making the choice to put my spirit in front of my ego. It's as simple as taking a breath in meditation. And just for the moment, I grasp having the creator and myself as one.

March 18th

Today is a day to practice being kind to ourselves. Our idea of living from wanting-to-wanting leads to more wanting. The notion of having leads to more having. Sometimes, if we're aware, we can realize we have so many thoughts running around in our heads and many of them are not helping us to be kind to ourselves.

The first step is to sit quietly in meditation, becoming aware of individual thoughts. Once we do that, then we can see several things. The first thing we can see is how many thoughts seem to be strung out on the line, like a mix of fresh and dirty laundry. The next thing we can see is that we do not have to change a thing about this – we can just sit and watch. After a while, we may see all of the thoughts labeled either good or bad. Here is where we can make a change. What if we didn't label them at all? What if we accepted them as thoughts pertaining only to our physical existence?

Have you ever seen someone sitting with one leg and foot jiggling up and down? Maybe we would label them as troubled, fearful, angry, or simply possessing a lot of nervous energy. This is compulsive thinking. Yet, the foot jiggling doesn't have to be labeled at all. Perhaps the best thing we can do is notice that it's happening. Then, we can stop, center ourselves, and sit quietly with the feelings that arise. Just like we would notice this jiggling of thoughts, the goal is not to stop the thoughts, but to accept that they're coming – one after the other. Then, without labeling them, the silent breath we add to the mix gently stops the train without any effort.

Our goal is not to have an empty mind. Our awareness of the thoughts, dropping them in a space of loving kindness, becomes the gentle ambition. The moments of silence and peace that result, however few in the beginning of practice, will take care of themselves. This is the start of being kinder to ourselves.

On some days this door will open wider than on other days. Again, just being aware is the goal, not how wide the door opens. When thinking takes the place of being, then that's the place of disease. Focusing on being takes work and we have the rest of our lives to practice.

Once we become conscious of our thoughts and we practice letting them go, we experience an instant of peace that can grow. This is the seed to germinate in the garden of tender-loving-kindness.

There is a severe outbreak of "vomarreah" (coined by my cubicle mates) on the compound. The administration finally decides to close the inmates inside their respective housing units for three days. Sudden projectile vomiting affects both of my cubicle mates. My thoughts are spread all over the place. I am trying to be empathetic to those being affected by the pandemic; however, I am feeling disconnected.

Going inward, I am dealing with the fact that I have bronchitis. I am in bed, but not with the affliction of the masses. As a result, I am having a hard time asking for help with my own illness. My thoughts are *"This isn't what everyone else has, so you can do without help. Don't bother anyone with your needs. They won't be seen as important."*

This internal dialogue has plagued me all of my life. This type of thinking is what put me in prison- chronically ruminating over how I can do with just a little bit less. Accepting this reflection, but not buying into it, severs the core of my biggest character defect – self-doubt.

Allowing myself to experience silence, with feelings in tow, I ask for help from others around me. One inmate gives me some chest rub. Another provides a few Halls menthol throat lozenges. I make myself a cup of hot tea and make the decision to appeal for medical help in the morning. I cannot predict the outcome of the query, but I can change my habit of always putting myself last and let go of the outcome.

March 19th

Labels, labels, labels! It is a lie that we become the color of our skin, a fatality of our childhood, our educational background, or even the language we speak daily. Society does not teach us this, but there is something deeper within us that can show us the process towards wisdom. The problem is, if we continue doing more and more, we never get to sit quietly long enough to get to the bottom of things – to see who we really are.

But we all have something in common. We can all look in the mirror and see the inventory of all we do, covering who we are beneath our bodies. When we comb our hair, brush our teeth, or wash our faces, we may not be aware that all human beings can see within themselves somewhere. It's like the perfectly wrapped Christmas package that we never choose to open. It's always under the tree, always fresh, and always a joyful mystery. But we have to look for it there.

Telling ourselves we don't have time, while in prison, to take stock of who we are is folly. We have plenty of time to look for the gift which is us, but it takes courage. The natural abilities within us may be buried under a mountain of overused words or actions, or hidden by anger, fear, guilt, and shame.

With faith in hand, we go looking for this gift of our being-ness slowly. And we have to do it alone. The more we think we're different from others, the further we move away from the discovery.

Once we get below the components of what we do, what we say, what we think, and what we feel, we come to know that all of us are connected to the endowment of who we are. There is no time involved. From the moment we're born, until we die, the secret is there to be discovered. All we have to do is be awake and come to know and listen – to be whole.

Besides who we are, when we open the box that says "today," it is even more important that we view the events from the perspective of which we are, rather than focus on reacting to what life's moments bring us. Who we are has a never-ending limit of possibilities. Here we find the endless love for being human. We can ask, "Are we connected right now?"

I found an inmate gifted in the ability to help me with the editing process of this book. I look upon the fear of asking him for help with acceptance and receive his contributions with great respect and awe.

Today, I make the human mistake of knocking on his door to give him the previous day's entry for refinement. What I do not see is his roommate asleep in the bunk below. I make a decision to leave the page on the top of his locker, since he does not respond to my gentle knock on his cabinet.

When I come later to deliver the story that goes with the abstract, he meets me with an incredible opportunity to just be – without labels. Unknown to me, I offended his sleeping roommate. The man did not come to me directly to solve the dilemma, however, I expressed a desire to clean up the mess and apologized to him directly.

Without judging the passive aggressive reaction of the man's discontent, I went to him to clean up my side of the street. Just dealing with the error at hand, I apologize for not noticing his sleeping presence. I acknowledge my humanity and also forgive him for his, without discussing anything with him directly. I'm not here to change him, only to accept what is; and when I am wrong, promptly admit it.

He gives me the very helpful suggestion of gently prodding the mattress to gain the attention of my newly found professor of grammar. That is the gift of today! I can receive help and get my needs met without being defensive in the process. I make a choice to go below the wrapping labels of what we do and address a character flaw that is keeping me from being peaceful.

March 20th

Time is something we're all serving, and yet, we share that with every human being in the world. Developing a spiritual relationship can change how we comprehend time. Rather than spending countless moments ruminating over past events or future prospects, developing the gentle discipline to live in the present moment of now is a practice that conquers the illusory passage of time.

Being conscious of our bodies, thoughts, emotions, and our interconnected life breath in a calm, ever-progressing, concentration of focus, leaves little time for the mind to wander. This doesn't happen overnight.

There is no passage of time in the spirit. Pure consciousness just is. What we encounter as sentient beings becomes bent and distorted by our ego-centered senses.

After lunch, sitting quietly on my bed, I realize that time can be treated like a meal. Once I've eaten it, digested it for its necessity, it's only a matter of hours before I have to eliminate the waste. Then, flush, it's gone – not another thought given. Whatever I'm eating is what I concentrate on. What would be the point of reminiscing about food from the past or what I will eat in the future? The lunch in front of me is the only important food to eat.

The level of consciousness coming to me seems even more open. As I open my mouth to receive the meal, I can see the act of shutting down my soul as a refusal to eat. Having the choice of attending to life as it comes to me is the real banquet. I've come to realize that prayer is nothing more than a conversation I'm having with the whole creation of The Universe. Meditation is just listening for awareness in return, without any expectation.

I write the following on a piece of paper and place it on my desk during the early weeks of my incarceration. "You may imprison my body, but you cannot subdue my soul." It remains free to assist me to grow and expand without limit, regardless of where I am housed."

Spending time alone gives me moments to set my mind to the side, to open my soul to life, kindness, compassion, and the love of peace that only comes from the still, quiet voice inside me.

The Universe really loves me. When I think about the past, it is I who have shut the door. I was taught to do so and the fact it became a habit is another thought I watch come and go. I know how to open myself by using present moment consciousness. I have the wisdom to open a portal to love because pain has occurred. I have to continue to make a decision to keep my spiritual senses open to receive the bounty of what life has to offer. Living in the present moment is the key process.

Life's difficult and challenging situations, cultivated in the rich soil of the present moment, will always have meaning and purpose waiting to be discovered. All I need do is add the water of willingness.

March 21st

We can act out of wisdom or we can react to things, people, places, and ideas. If we're not sure about the wisdom of what to do or not do, we can become aware of what we feel. Are we afraid, angry, lonely, ashamed, or even joyful? Once we know what we feel, then the real miracle of understanding starts to emerge. But first, we have to be awake and open to who we are.

Who we are is not what we feel or what we do. Once we accept those facts, the wisdom of who we are, whether alive on this earth, or free from our bodies after death, is timeless and constant. All we have to do is create a habit of sitting quietly with ourselves long enough to understand this vision.

Using this discipline of living in the present moment, we can use the complementary relationship between distinctly separate feeling states and the mindful observer of who we are. We only react when we believe what we feel is permanent. Wisdom teaches us that feelings come and go, just the same as every passing moment.

The only thing constant is our breath. Here is where we become anchored to who we are. This is where we come to accept the passage of time, making better choices in each moment.

To change the focus from the impermanent, what we do to who we are, takes courage and daily commitment. What we do from moment to moment now depends on the wider view of how it affects the whole Universe, not one individual over the other. We are all bound to the who-we-are of creation. That's serene wisdom. It is an illusion that we think and feel differently from one another. The only constancy is that everything changes and passes.

We're all in this together, whether we like it or not. When we face what we don't like, there is a chance to journey

inside ourselves – to eat the false ego of who we think we are and let it dissolve.

God, grant me the serenity to accept the things I cannot change, the courage to change the things I can, and the wisdom to know the difference.

This is the simplest, most non-religious, prayer I know. The words haven't changed, but I have evolved to embrace it in a new and different way over the years. Today, it is all about listening and watching, creating a sufficient pause to see more clearly how to act on the energy of wisdom.

Someone I know went to watch TV in the adjoining dayroom. I avoid that room like the plague. I find it to be a place of total selfish unconsciousness. Someone kicked a chair in which a man was sitting and shouted in Spanish. "You're in my f—king seat!" The man rose, flailing his arms in disbelief, and the Latin "shot-caller" (a leader of one of the Hispanic gangs) popped him in the cheek. My buddy reared back with his reaction, and without any hesitation, cracked the assailant back with his fist in the neck.

I listen very carefully to the description of the specifics of the disagreement, while I am in the middle of my afternoon meditation. I don't interfere with the discussion. I am not searching for the wisdom to impart to my friend. I am absorbing the information to enrich my own incorporeal walk.

In silence, on the breath, here is what wisdom teaches me:

- The shot-caller had to react to my friend's presence of sitting in "his chair".
- Both men responded before they thought about the repercussions of their gut reactions.
- The assailant was surprised that my friend defended himself. As the shot-caller, he was not used to being challenged.
- The incident furthered my belief that the TV room is a place of total selfish unconsciousness.

This tale has a happy ending. The shot-caller apologized for his indiscretion. My friend didn't further the escalation by pushing the issue.

What I learned, from listening today, was to continue valuing meditation as a way of making better decisions, giving me the space to gather more than just a reflexive response. I'm in prison because I didn't see the larger picture.

March 22nd

What is pain for? We may keep asking ourselves this question. Perhaps we have done so for many years. Why did I have a troubled childhood? The deeper we look at these types of discussions, the darker it gets. The darker it gets, the more complaining we do. The more we complain, the more our attitudes color various moments of our day. While sitting quietly, doing my best to let go of the current self-talk, I come upon a very simple answer in a brief instance of silence.

Maybe, for a while, this answer doesn't make any sense. Then Bam! The wall of ignorance falls down. This is part of the cycle of life. The Universe wishes to experience life through us in this way. We can stop blaming ourselves and start listening to the simple voice of our spirits. From birth, we have experienced growing pains all the way through the point of adulthood. But our spiritual growth is meant to continue taking us down the path we are supposed to travel.

As we sit in prison, we have a unique opportunity to observe ourselves in a whole new way. Just as autumn turns into winter and winter into spring, we can develop a style to watch and befriend ourselves as our lives wane and wax from season to season. We can witness the creation of new buds for growth in a time of emotionally cold darkness. We can practice being with ourselves and turning loneliness into solitude. We can become our own best friends.

We don't have to fight or judge the constant unpleasant noise, angry outbursts, or the lack of what our egos want over and over. This can be a time to sit and practice self-kindness, real compassion, and inner peace. We have the time to alter our perspective and to stop taking things so personally. By doing so, we develop less of a desire to cling to all the pleasures our personalities yearn for.

We can sit with the discomfort of what we term pain, only to realize it's a natural occurrence of the changing of a

season. Leaning into the grief of what is can create new strength.

We can stumble blindly and painfully down the road of life or we can choose to see a more joyous connection, as we open our spirits to a never-ending supply of wisdom. Perfection is not the goal – it's being a part of the whole.

I developed a respiratory illness during the outbreak of an ugly gastrointestinal flu that confined us all to our units. I was bedridden for five days. During this time, I asked for help with this condition, without any accommodation.

Knowing my own character defect of self-doubt, I continue to ask for help – even though my natural reaction is to sit with my fear and endure my malaise.

The situation comes to a head when the compound is opened back up and inmates are asked to return to work. I am still not over my illness. I do not feel well enough to return to work. The voice in my head rings loud and clear: *"My opinion, as an inmate, is not valued in the larger scheme of health concerns."* (This is a thought worth releasing.) I express my anger by slamming my locker door before heading to the responsibilities for the day.

Once at work, there is no place for me to sit and care for myself. I lie down on a cart, but am soon asked to leave work. Push comes to shove and I am ordered to medical. I am given treatment prescriptions, but no antibiotics. I am also not given any further time off from work.

I spend the rest of the day doing my best not to take this incident personally, especially since the physician exclaimed, during the examination, “We don’t do compassion here, just healthcare.” Compassion and kindness has to come from inside. I have to go to the space to release my discontent and my listlessness.

I take the medication they prescribe, practicing gratitude, and continue my regimen of finding peace within. This situation is a moment of winter and is not going to disconnect me from the evolution of all of my seasons of experience.

March 23rd

Other people's opinions of me are none of my business. This is easier to say, than it is to practice. We must have faith in grace, while expanding our spirits as our primary source of inspiration. Then, we have to "act as if" (in the physical world) until creation happens. The more we innovate with The Universe, the more love fills our cup. Consequently, love can run over to distribute to others. The Buddhists call this tonglen. Christians call it charity. It matters not what we call it, but that we become human beings who can avoid grasping substance.

Life brings on a more meaningful purpose for us, as well as those whose path we touch. Other people can never know who we are, but if we know, then we intuitively understand the connection to the whole. Our egos have opinions that can create a constant, compulsive, inner dialogue of negativity. It's usually wrong. Learning to place our spiritual part in front of our egos allows us to watch our lives consciously. Through this cutting edge focus, we develop greater power and truth.

If I worry about what people are saying behind my back, or stress over the dissatisfaction they express to my face, I give them the power to control how I feel, how I see myself, and how I act out the moments, hours, and days of my life. I can either live a soap opera life, with silly commercials, or choose to live a full length documentary worthy of an Academy Award nomination. It is my choice.

Before writing, I spend a short time breathing in the source of love from wherever it comes in the Universe without definition. The importance is to open my heart to the possibility of tender-loving-kindness. Then, I exhale the love I receive outward towards other people through a long stream of meditation.

Some people are very close to me, while others are only passing by in my field of peripheral vision. The hardest part of my practice concerns the people my ego insists on calling enemies. I breathe in the pain and send out compassion to them anyway, because those enlightened before me suggested I give it a while and experience it for myself. It is their opinion my ego fears the most. But this is folly.

This practice shows me so much light. First, I soak in as much love as my soul can hold. Yet, I don't hold on to it. I breathe it outward and give it away. When I do this for my supposed enemies, it heals the dark parts within me that push away love. I find these adversaries represent the parts of me that I don't allow love to enter. By forgiving them, I forgive myself. I begin to understand how we are all connected.

After meditating, I look outside my window to see the grass, clover, and dandelions that are starting to sprout in the yard. I see a honey bee laboring hard over the wildflowers to gather what is needed for a day's work. This is a view from my spirit – not from my short-sighted, selfish ego.

I catch a glimpse of the sun coming out from behind a cloud. The cell is bathed in a bright light and I stop writing to look around the room. This isn't a coincidence. For a moment, the Universe is responding to what I am creating on paper. As I breathe out joy and pick up my pencil, the clouds cover the sun. I sense the cyclical order of things and I feel peaceful. Listening to my soul is more satisfying than anyone else's opinion of me.

March 24th

With larger eyes, let us be here with gentleness and compassion towards ourselves. With that expanded outlook, we can see more honestly, without our defenses. It is not all of society that treats us so poorly, but our narrow view of victimhood that rises falsely within us.

Once we are honest, kind and compassionate before the whole Universe, we can make the decision to let go and move on to the next moment. We don't slam the door on the past. Neither would we wish to relive those moments over and over, once we have faced the whole truth.

We have learned to lean headlong into the pain we have feared the most. We have invited this torment to sit right beside us without judgment. We have removed every whirling thought that gathers in our minds, that strengthens the hell inside us. We come to sit, even for an instant, in forgiving silence that comes with living fully in the present moment. This is our practice.

I face today with many thoughts that can mask developing my practice of self-forgiveness. Someone tells me something, while I am trying to be helpful, that totally pisses me off. But I refrain from saying the popular phrase, "Man, that shit's crazy." I recognize what is happening, realize what is trying to throw me off course, while my healing is in progress. Another person exclaims, "This meal sucks, especially the salad dressing." I am cognizant of expanding to the concept that there are some places in this world where many people are eating a lot less than we will be served today.

I'm well aware of the words the others repeat many times throughout the day. I ask myself, *"When do I use words that are helpful or hurtful in the long run?"* There are so many directions to go, but I have to widen what I see. The encouragement I seek comes from my faith within. I tend to see it, after I do it. Then, I understand it.

The compulsive chatter in my mind is another destructive force. These thoughts defend me, but they also fuel the painful feelings I am trying to solve. Then, I remember feelings aren't solved. They resolve in silence.

I heard about a hiker who came upon a butterfly struggling to escape its cocoon. Wishing to relieve the insect of its apparent pain, he whipped out his pocket knife, and with the greatest intentions of kindness, cut into its cocoonal prison, attempting to usher in an early release. But the traveler learned a valuable lesson that day. The act of squeezing out of its spun tomb was nature's way of pushing all the necessary fluids into the butterfly's new wings. Premature removal left the butterfly with crumpled, inoperative limbs. Unable to fly, it walked away clumsily and died within a few hours.

Life has a design. Trying to figure it out creates more madness for me. Trying to control life makes for hell on Earth. I'm currently in my own cocoon, surrounded by a lot of pain. The solution is never found outside. The question I ask myself is, *"How much time will I spend alone, squeezing out my wings, so when my time is up, I can fly away?"*

March 25th

Start today with the idea of a cloudless, blue sky that seems to go on forever. Now imagine sitting upon the highest mountain and looking out at the same view. Now sit and watch. Let the clouds roll in one at a time, but keep your perspective on the sky. Those clouds and the developing storms are the faults and shortcomings in our lives. It may be hard to look at them. We may feel ourselves suffering, as we attempt to pull away in pain.

Now, remember the sky. Go past it. Go on past the moon, the sun, the solar system, and on to the edge of the galaxy. All of this huge space exists outside of us. The same space exists inside us as well, but we have to go and find it. Perhaps it is the pain we feel that starts this journey outward and inward. Instead of clearly seeing the discomfort, our natural tendency is to push away from the table of now. We don't want this meal in front of us. But, if we sit and open ourselves to the experience, we can start to see that which is painful exists in a larger field, surrounded by love, compassion, and kindness.

A moment from the past: I remember the first time I became over-confident. It was after learning to ride my bicycle. I came crashing down onto the street, tearing up my knees and elbows. My shorts were no protection. I ran home with blood running down my legs and arms. But next, there was a warm bath to wash away the blood and a gentle soap to remove the small imbedded stones and dirt. Afterwards, there was a generous application of stinging Merthiolate to disinfect.

Finally, large gauze pads were applied with first aid tape, gently covering the wounds, creating the environment to heal. Isolating the accepted damage allowed for slow healing, along with protection from any future infection. The exercise became my acceptance of the discomfort of my skinned body, in addition to the experience of a gentle, soothing care complete with compassion and tenderness.

After a few days, the third leg of my process entered my wisdom mind. The pain was no longer there. It wasn't as permanent, as I had originally led myself to believe. I can still draw on this lesson today. I can see how time is fleeting. It has been decades since that moment; however, I realize that this present moment will pass into emptiness as well.

Now that I have this larger perspective, I can see time and space as vivid in the moment; yet it is also dead, as it as it is replaced by the next moment and the next. Life is impermanent, but I can draw on this kindness and compassion that has no end. I must deal honestly and directly with the reality of life, both the moments of sunshine and of rain. I surround myself with love, charity, and the openness of space and time that can heal.

The line-servers were short one person, so I agreed to set up the trays for dinner. Passing the serving plate to the person and distributing a bag of potato chips is easy. But this is prison. Nothing is ever easy for long.

An inmate approaches and says, “Gimme a bag of chips.” I reply, “I can’t.” He is demanding an extra bag. I can’t afford to lose my job, as this it provides the money I survive on. He becomes angry, swearing, trying to make me responsible for his emotion. “You ain’t the po-lice. You in jail.” Frankly, this phrase is overused. He’s in jail too!

Thinking about this dilemma doesn’t solve the problem. Acting in silence does. I have to be the cloudless sky. I just let him pass by with his resentment, affirming whatever healing can take place in the moment. He isn't happy that God is in command of my will.

That evening, I go to the store guy on the unit and buy a bag of chips. I take it to the man who wanted them earlier. I present them to him. He receives the gesture poorly. He isn't going to take the bag. This is not part of his plan.

I make a decision to be the sky. What difference does it make where the snack comes from? He continues to be defiant of my gesture. I explain that I'm acting out the writing of this book. "Please take this generosity." I offer the gift again. He takes the bag without a word. Now he is silent. Interesting!

March 26th

"Bang! Let's begin today with the concept of the beginning of the Universe. First, there was nothing. Then, scientists tell us there was this huge explosion hundreds of billions of years ago. Now, let's go to the moment where something started from nothing. Right there! There's a relationship between the nothingness and the "something-ness." It's fresh, new, untouched by flaw. There are no labels. It is much more basic than even the uniting of sperm and egg. More basic than the start of a human being.

Now, arise with exactly the same freshness. Start with any breath. Be conscious. Breathe in and exhale. For some, that's Genesis. For Christians, it is being born again in the Holy Spirit. For the Muslims, it is the time taken to pause in prayer during the day. The Buddhists choose sitting in silence to become aware of the "self" beyond the constant chatter of our minds. Being conscious is faith in action. Life can start over at any chosen breath, leaving behind the previous breath as a dream. Each moment can be a big bang, but only if we choose to create that increment of being awake with every respiration.

We can start to see an appearance of our unknowingness. Are we something or nothing? Which one shall we choose? Are we a physical body with a spiritual foundation, or are we a spiritual awareness inside a physical body? Most likely, we find this question unanswerable. Being human is a paradox. We are both spiritual and physical. We are neither and both. Again, the key to serenity, in this relationship, is starting fresh. Starting at the same point that started it all. Recreate that moment and find the peace there.

The practical way of experiencing the big bang daily is to choose a time to sit still. This is very difficult in prison. Much of the day, and even the night, is filled with banging, flushing, and yelling. I have found a period right after breakfast when there is a lull. This is my individual situation.

My aim is to quiet my body and my mouth. Once I've done that, and I breathe, I am faced with the 'Big Bang' of the compulsive conversation in my mind. My goal is not to silence this chatter. That's like trying to stop the explosion of creation. I just observe it's happening and go back to the beginning, with the emptiness of starting over with my breath.

If I don't experience a train of monumental noiselessness, I just accept that and start over. The goal is not to hush the clamber, but to be aware and with my breath. If I find myself thinking up a storm, I just go back to the moment before the big bang and say "thinking." Then, I start over. Each time I begin again, I continue to go back to the point of awareness that parallels the starting of the Universe.

I am not here to master this method. I am only willing to practice it and let go. I do this at least once daily, but sometimes as much as four times. I experience the habit of starting over with a fresh, expanded, less cluttered space than ever before. This path has not been a straight line. My path is different and unique to me.

March 27th

Native Americans say, "Judge not a man until you have walked a mile in his moccasins." This is an important step to free ourselves from the narrowing power of selfish ego. When we put ourselves in search of the viewpoints of others, we begin the process of understanding true compassion. We all have egos. We all fall prey to our own selfishness. No one escapes opinions or feelings.

The compassion we develop by looking at life through another person's eyes can soften our own harsh criticism. We're brought closer to others by empathizing with the pain and the joy we share in common. We all have the same doubts, fears, anger, sadness, and loneliness. Rather than getting bogged down in hiding from all of this perceived darkness, compassion becomes a beacon that we can share outwardly.

Imagine being in a large, darkened field with thousands of people. You are in the pitch of night, under a heavy cloud cover. There is no moon. No stars provide the light of faith, hope, or love. Now put yourself in the hearts and minds of all those around you in that somberness. There is only a hollow breeze and silence. Imagine the fear, the loneliness, and the separateness that each of us feels in zero visibility. Feel the tremendous need of all the people.

Now reach into your pocket and pull out your own candle of compassion. Light it to pierce the darkness. Out of the spiritual component that binds us together, encourage the person next to you to risk allowing you to light their candle. Pass the flame of hope in every possible direction. Now wait and watch. Each person has the choice to reach to the front, back, left, and right - to pass a light that connects. A single flame grows to dozens, growing faster and larger, until the whole field is illuminated with the light of grace.

Soak in all that luminosity. If someone's flame goes out accidentally, someone close by relights their candle and faith is restored.

Now imagine standing in the field, asking everyone to extinguish their flames. The whole field is plunged back into blackness. The awkwardness of fear and disconnection returns. Then, reach into your pocket again. Light your candle. Pass the light along. In a fresh moment, the darkness is driven back by the growing light of passing torches.

When we first learn the wisdom of feeling and expressing compassion, it becomes easier to create hope again – whenever there is a need. Perhaps, this is the mystery of the second coming of Christ. At any moment, when there is real lack, we use a fresh start, rather than judging one another. We give what we know truthfully. It pierces the darkness of hopelessness and despair. The second coming of compassion can be recreated by being awake, then acting.

I share today's entry with my victim impact class. The topic is supposed to relate to the development of self-esteem. I pose the following question: *Am I spending my days wallowing in my own darkness and creating self-hatred, while alone in my cube?* We must open our heart and see that others are suffering. I light the flame of compassion for myself first. Then, I deliver it to another. This is not a single occurrence. Over time, there will be many opportunities for a second coming, each following every possible, present moment. I am aware of my breath. I light my flame anew.

March 28th

Glenda, the Good Witch of the North (from "The Wizard of Oz"), said, "It's always best if we start at the beginning." This wisdom statement applies to us, as well, every day. When we open up and love ourselves from the perspective of who we are, we will run into the roadblock of all of the things we have said and done, in our lifetimes. The things that have paved the way for suffering – both within ourselves and others.

We can look at Dorothy and her adventures with the scarecrow, the tin man, and the cowardly lion. In reality, they are reflections of our own humanity. She practices grace within the shortcomings of all three of the other characters. In helping them, she helps herself because her companions are merely counterparts of her inward self. The pseudo-truth of separateness is an illusion.

The prefix, "co" has a root meaning of togetherness. Passion is the experience of understanding the painful struggle in life. Practicing mercy starts from within and then can be extended to others because we can relate.

Opening up to any pain we experience, whether created or received, is a courageous act. Compassion heals from the soul, without judgment or fault finding. The soul knows no fault because there is only one soul to which we either choose to connect or not. Sides do not exist in the spiritual realm. All we have to do is breathe inward and start over at any time. If something goes wrong, we can acknowledge it and start over in the present moment.

The more I judge others, the more harshly I lash out at myself. Being conscious acknowledges and loves the whole. It reminds me of a humorous story I once heard:

All the parts of the body got together to discuss what part was supreme. The brain started by touting its superior intellect. Without the brain's direction, nothing would happen. The heart interrupted to proclaim that without its ability to circulate the blood and to feel love for the body, there would be no enjoyment in life. The hands and the legs then fought over which was more valuable. Was it the ability to walk from place to place, or the ability to write, touch, and get things done? The lungs took a deep breath and bellowed without them the body would have no way of creating life's breath.

The more one body part proclaimed its superiority, the more the other parts grew louder. There ensued quite an uproar. Then, the anus opened and started to proclaim its worth. There was a small amount of silence. Then, all the parts of the body began to laugh in unison, calling it smelly and worthless.

The anus became enraged and decided to teach the rest of the body a lesson. It shut down and would let nothing pass. Soon the body began to fill up with waste. The brain became dizzy. The lungs panted heavily, as the heart started skipping beats, the legs faltered, and the arms had no strength to keep the body from falling to the ground. The asshole held its turf, until every part surrendered to its importance.

Then, the asshole proclaimed, "We all have our function and our service to the flesh. We are all equal. We need to remember we are bound to work together for the greater good." With that, all the body parts sighed with relief to a lesson learned. All returned to a normal function.

We all have good and bad within. We all deserve compassion as a result. We can forgive ourselves. We forgive others, as we wish to be forgiven. This dynamic includes everyone. Even the most evil character has an opportunity to pass commiseration in both directions. We can no longer afford to think of ourselves as alone. Wars are created out of self-righteousness.

Just for today, I can choose to focus on three simple elements, as I carry out my day:

- Be more conscious of who or what I regard with disgust and greed.
- Make a decision to open up to the space where tender-loving-kindness comes from within.
- Once filled to the brim, I can elect to pass compassion to anyone I meet, whether they have it in return or not.

March 29th

Today we can spend some time being aware of what attracts us and draws us closer— whether it is a person, place, thing, feeling or state. Pleasure is something we naturally move toward. We can also spend time being aware of what we avoid. Now, we can go a step further and become familiar with that which we normally ignore. What are we missing while we are absorbed with ourselves?

By looking at what brings us pleasure, pain, and ignorance, we can create an awareness to grow personally. We are learning not to suppress any emotions, nor to act them out in the world and create more suffering for ourselves and The Universe.

Genuine peace comes from accepting exactly what is happening in the moment. We don't have to like it. We can be honest about our feelings without reacting to them. We may struggle a bit to find this acceptance and peace. Nevertheless, we have an opportunity to trust in this wisdom. We only have to sit still with what we feel, until a universal revelation comes to us in its own time.

I was put into Administrative Segregation again without notice or reason. I stayed there two weeks before I was asked to sign a separation agreement. I decided to use this moment to grow. What are the three parameters of my situation?

- I am attracted to leaving this isolation cell, to having my freedom, to being in regular population. I crave having what my ego wants.

- I'm pushing away from the hurt. I think I was punished without a conversation. I have no idea who did this to me. I'm thinking too much.
- I'm ignorant of all the missing pieces that allow me to be peaceful. Asking why only drives me to either obsessive thoughts of pleasure to feed the anger and hurt justified by my ego. The best question I might ask in silence is. *"What else am I overlooking?"* I have to widen my scope.

To reach peace and joy, I must accept that I am here in this cell and sit with what I feel. I am working on allowing the three categories of pleasure, pain, and ignorance to bring me to a new sense of spiritual maturity. I'm no saint, but I can use this situation as an opportunity to get closer to who I am and away from my ego. I can lean into discomfort and develop the courage to be a warrior of great internal strength.

Finally, right in the middle of what I usually tend to totally ignore, there are seeds of wisdom from which I can draw some strength. I would have missed the joy of the chicken tenders that are being served for dinner. They are delicious. I can touch that briefly in my mind and then let it go. Just for the moment, I open my heart to the discomfort, while being gentle and affirming to myself without the need to cling to my wants. I must be willing to continue to remain open, expanding my courage to the vast possibilities of which I am unaware today.

In sitting, I breathe in the pain and breath out the peace of what is not yet realized. I start with myself and then extend to all who feel this way in the moment. Feeling the connection, when I practice, is a simple service to the whole.

Hindsight is always 20/20. I was moved to an institution with so much to offer my spiritual development. The number of mental, physical, and self-improvement classes and programs is extensive, compared to where I was. The most important thing I can do is stay present to whatever comes to my consciousness. Whatever happens in a year probably won't be significant. To test this hypothesis, I go back a year and try to remember the details of the whole day. Enough said.

March 30th

Society seems very interested in educating the masses. Even while in prison, there are structural programs to help inmates start over wherever they are. There are programs to secure a GED. Vocational training is available in many places. The emphasis seems to be on mental knowledge, or IQ (Intelligence Quotient). We can ask the question, "Does that really improve us in a way everyone benefits?" What is not taught in school is real wisdom. We might call that EQ (Emotional Quotient).

Beginning with our own inventory, we must look for this wisdom with clear-sighted honesty. The first fundamental truth to practice is a gentle, kind, compassionate approach to the journey. This is one of the amazing benefits of meditation.

Remember the story of the tortoise and the hare? Slow and steady wins the race. This innate wisdom, over intelligence, provides the key understanding to the phrase, "A chain is only as strong as its weakest link."

We can draw on other areas of our lives to improve our EQ. When we go to the gym, a dedicated athlete will tell us, "No pain, no gain." Keeping the idea of a gentle approach in mind, we can bring our focus to this concept. There are two ways to exercise our emotional growth. It begins with sending and receiving basic emotional states, without the mind becoming "interruptive." Secondly, as soon as we start to evaluate a situation, either positive or negative, and our mind/ego starts to take over, we can make a decision to go straight to the heart. Here we treat pain and pleasure as something to observe, rather than respond reflexively.

Making a commitment to use our breath to guide our emotional growth is wisdom in action. Now we can work with pain and pleasure in our new exercise program, keeping in mind the lessons already learned in the physical gym. As we breathe in what is painful, we sit with the weight of the

darkness. Just before breathing out, we open our hearts to the discomfort, and with a wider faith, we breathe out a broader solution that will come in its own time to increase our insight.

Now I can take myself to a larger view by breathing in the same pain I am currently experiencing – even with anyone close by who is having the same uneasiness. The specifics don't matter. My mind focuses and I choose to drop the thinking process. It's not my team vs. your team. I become a part of those with the same painful emotional viewpoint, with compassion and kindness driving the moment of healing discernment.

With each breath, I venture out to a larger and larger group, until I am engulfed in a relationship with the whole world. Your pain is my pain and my pain is yours. I can see this moment connecting us, instead of convoluting separation. What I wish for myself, I wish for others. The wisdom is that there is no break in the connection perceived by my mind. Selfishness constricts me and echoes the pain. I can see a dog forever chasing its tail. A tail it never reaches. When I accept emotional pain and observe, it dissolves in my understanding.

What brings me enjoyment can be treated in the same wise fashion. I breathe in the symphony of gladness. Then, I breathe it out for others to enjoy. My ego says to hold onto it, but I'm reminded I'm in the emotional gym and training for a marathon. I don't hold onto the joy, as my ego urges. I briefly see and feel the pleasure for what it is, then I start sending it to those I love dearly. With each breath inward and outward, I can increase the scope to friends, everyday people on the compound, and even to my enemies.

Sending joy out to my enemies is not going to fly right away. I have to "fake it 'til I make it". For me, this is an underdeveloped emotional muscle. I have found wisdom creeps in slowly. Something inside me changes when I wish to give contentment to those that conjure up fear and anger against me. Now, the darkness within me, where no openness or daylight has pierced for years, begins to unfold to a newfound sense of relief. In loving my enemies, I come to love all of myself. My neighbor and I are all connected in view of this experience. When I am kind to others, being compassionately aware, I am becoming my own best friend.

March 31st

When faced with a situation that brings out the worst in us, we can also be given time to expand our growth as spiritual human beings. Concepts like this can be used to open our eyes and to wake up. All we have to do is make a decision to be aware and see all that is possible to comprehend. Normally, we just react! Now is the perfect occasion to look at problems with a broader appreciation.

When we do what we have always done, we get what we have always gotten. Change involves acting our way into a new way of being. We need two things to achieve this new action – willingness and a practice period. We cannot run any distance, until we first tie our shoes.

It's close to 3 a.m. Suddenly, in the hollow stillness of the night, an inmate starts to sing loudly. His voice echoes off of every wall. Perhaps there might be a shred of pleasantry, but he is not only boisterous, he's also painfully out of tune. Ok! It's time to get grounded! I can repress any feelings I have. I put tissue paper in my ears, then wrap a towel around my head. I could go to the door and blurt out my reaction to his madness.

Instead, I sit briefly and breathe in my annoyance. I can see it clearly and honestly. Harm is being done, not only to me, but to anyone who is trying to sleep. Acknowledging the pain, with acceptance, is the goal. He keeps on singing, wailing louder and louder. Of course, someone else loses patience and yells, “Shut the f—k up!” Perhaps there are others repressed in silence, not wishing to exhort their opinion on the matter. I decide to use a meditation technique to see what I can learn.

I steer away from any acting-out response, but include the other inmate’s reaction in my practice. For all those repressing or wanting to act-out, I breathe in the pain and breathe out the sentiment of compassion from my heart. Then, I breathe in the pain of the singing itself (being out of tune) and the harm that is being inflicted on everyone in the unit. I breathe out compassion and kindness for myself, all the others, and also for the inmate who is singing.

After several minutes of breathing in the adversity and breathing out an expanded empathy toward everyone in the incident, I sit quietly to listen to any response that might arise within me. I drop any opinions of thought and just give space to the moment, opening to wisdom.

Several points of discernment come to light in my heart:

- Eventually, this out-of-tune crooner will tire and stop. He cannot go on forever. This is like a thunderstorm that will eventually pass.

- This is an opportunity for me to increase my ability to grow in patience and understanding. The larger view is coming.

- The inmates have a right to acknowledge the annoyance. What does it help to scream at the inmate? He only gets louder.

- Now is the time to open the space and drop the anger – mine and all of the other suffering inmates. In its place, breathing out compassion fills the need of the hole created by the pain. I can breathe out this awareness to everyone affected.

- Now is the time to open the space of my breath to the singing inmate. What discomfort is he feeling that drives him to bellow out his sour tune in this early morning hour? I cannot answer that question– that is thinking. I need to stick with my heart. Instead, I focus on compassion for the pain he is suffering. Finally, I breathe out the compassion of forgiveness for myself and the singer. Why? Because I can admit to doing selfish acts to soothe my own suffering, unaware of how it is received by others. By forgiving and being compassionate to him, I am forgiving that dark space in my own heart that needs understanding and light. I breathe out that same wisdom for everyone on the unit.

- I keep breathing in the pain, breathing out compassion and kindness for the whole world. Since we're all connected by who we are as feeling human beings, I am able to further heal and forgive myself by expanding as far as I could go. I use this experience to become more enlightened. And then, there is silence. I drift back to sleep, peacefully restored.

SERIES INFO

Thank you so much for completing *Growth*, *An Inmate's Guide to Corrections*, which is Book One in a Four-Book Series. To continue your experience, please access the next three books in the series!

ALL FOUR BOOKS IN THE SERIES

BOOK ONE:	**Growth, An Inmate's Guide to Corrections** **January 1st through March 31st**
BOOK TWO:	**Sustain, An Inmate's Guide to Corrections** **April 1st through June 30th**
BOOK THREE:	**Decay, An Inmate's Guide to Corrections** **July 1st through September 30th**
BOOK FOUR:	**Solitude, An Inmate's Guide to Corrections** **October 1st through December 31st**

About the Author

At 60 years old, Craig Byrnes is a first-time author, residing in Washington, D.C. This book was crafted while serving a federally mandated 40-month sentence at a low security correctional facility.

So, what's a man to do when he learns he's going to be incarcerated for a lengthy amount of time? There are choices. He can continue living in the same cycle of mental and spiritual paths that put him there. Or, he can choose to face all facets of his life, learn to forgive, to let go and to move forward into a place of validation.

Bad things happen – even to good people. Yet, EVERYONE has the potential within for tragedy to be transformed.

My Tragedy

I told a story to a man named George. I have to own this story, although it's not a pretty one. But, more importantly, the tale I wove was not true. I told a fairytale to make both myself and someone else feel important.

What I didn't realize was the fact that George told the authorities my fabricated story - and then some. By calling me, sometime later, to confirm the (fake) details I had supplied, he was able to get his own sentence reduced for a real crime. I was arrested and jailed. In taking the advice of others, I plead guilty to a lesser charge in an effort to get the entire ordeal behind me. I think it's imperative to note the assumptions the authorities made about me (and my perceived deeds) have never materialized.

Which brings us back to the question: What's a man to do when he learns he's going to be incarcerated for an extended period of time?

A very dear, spiritual friend started to send me books about a more intense form of meditation practice. He suggested I start reading, while awaiting my sentencing. After thousands of hours of practice, the wisdom that came to me wasn't really about prison life, although incarceration played a huge part. The larger, intrinsic lesson was the necessity of learning how to conquer old life patterns, practice forgiveness, and move forward to a place of self-validation.

I continue to use this book daily. I have rebuilt my entire life through these practices. I'm not perfect and don't expect to be. But, I'm grateful for my time of incarceration. If the consequences of my life had not stacked up in a way to force me to look inward, I doubt I would have my inner peace. I hope you do not have to go through anything similar to obtain your own inner peace. Perhaps this book can help with your journey.

Should you have any questions, thoughts or comments, feel free to email me at: craig@inmatesguidetocorrections.com. I look forward to hearing from you!

CPSIA information can be obtained
at www.ICGtesting.com
Printed in the USA
LVHW081629170420
653830LV00017B/3593

9 781986 008044